Vegetable Gardening

Made Easy

28 27 26 25 24   1 2 3 4 5

ISBN: 978-0-7603-8150-2

Digital edition published in 2024
eISBN: 978-0-7603-8151-9

Library of Congress Cataloging-in-Publication Data is available.

Design and page layout: Tanya Jacobson
Cover Image: Jessica Hendrix Puff
Photography: see Photo Credits on page 186
Back cover image: Resh Gala

Printed in China

Vegetable Gardening
Made Easy

Simple Tips & Tricks
to Grow Your Best
Garden Ever

Resh Gala

COOL
SPRINGS
PRESS

INTRODUCTION

My Story

It took me time to appreciate that gardening is more than planting a seed and hoping for a harvest. It's a skill, a passion, and a pursuit in perseverance—and is now the story of my life.

One day while out shopping with my family, I decided to buy two tomato plants from a big box retailer on a whim—and failed miserably to grow anything. I couldn't understand how a girl from Jersey couldn't grow Jersey tomatoes! That was the day that my gardening journey began—with questions in my mind and an obsession to understand how growing food could be so hard (it is not, I promise you) when eating food is so easy.

After the tomato fiasco, the next year, I decided to hire a landscaper to build four small raised beds for me (2 feet × 3 feet or 61 cm × 91 cm each). Little did I know that the beds were filled with topsoil from a construction site, devoid of nutrients and with actual rocks in them. Once again, I was disappointed with the problems in the garden. (All the pests and diseases came to feast on my unhealthy plants, of course!) But I learned something extremely valuable from that experience—that good soil was the absolute foundation of a healthy, thriving garden, and as an added bonus, I now had the ability to recognize all the garden pests in the world (well almost). Once I replaced my soil and started adding homemade compost to my beds, the change was most dramatic. Plants started to thrive, pests almost disappeared, and bountiful harvests began to come fast and strong!

What I'm trying to say is that so many of us give up on the first attempt, often saying that we don't have a green thumb. A bit of education, a bit of adventure, and some dogged determination is likely to lead to spectacular results . . . as it did for me.

Today, I have thousands of followers on Instagram @reshgala and run my own organic gardening business called Hundred Tomatoes LLC (birthed from my love of tomatoes and an ode to my gardening journey). We design, consult, install, and maintain beautiful and productive organic vegetable gardens in New Jersey and around the US. Our mission is to encourage people to grow their own food and live their best lives.

Resh working in her fall/winter garden.

Resh with her massive backyard harvest.

About This Book

My whole purpose in writing this book is to help you become a better gardener, instill a love of growing food, taking the confusion away so you can enjoy bountiful harvests while feeling a sense of accomplishment and empowerment that you grew your own food.

All the tips, tricks, and techniques found in this book are presented in the simplest way possible and will take your garden game from GOOD TO GREAT! Most of us live busy, demanding lives and want instant gratification, answers, and results. This book will deliver just that—with quick, easy, bite-sized solutions to your most common yet confusing vegetable gardening questions.

At the end of the day, I want you to remember one thing: That when it comes to gardening, there are absolutely no hard and fast rules, no right or wrong way to grow something—just **your** way of growing things that brings you joy, peace, and happiness.

Create a garden space that's both productive and captivating, which will bring joy into your life.

Chapter 1

DESIGN & PLAN THE GARDEN

Growing your own food is one of the most rewarding and joyful things in life. However, planning what to grow and where to grow it is not easy. Just head to your local nursery or garden center and it's easy to be overwhelmed by the choices. There are so many different seed packets, varieties of herbs and vegetables, soil options, and on and on. At home, you might be scratching your head about picking the right location for your vegetable garden, building your raised beds, or filling them with the best soil.

Planning, designing, and laying out the garden are crucial steps. You want it to be right the first time so you can avoid the headaches of a do-over. Think of your organic edible garden as an extension of your home and personality—you want your garden to look beautiful, be productive, and last for many years to come. Lay a solid foundation and you will avoid problems down the road. Have a vision for your garden. You want enough space to be able to grow food and move around comfortably between your raised beds. You also want to have space to move a wheelbarrow too and possibly have a seating area where you can relax and entertain. You may even want to leave extra room for an expansion in the future.

This chapter includes quick, easy tips on planning and designing your vegetable garden layout, creating productive planting plans to maximize your harvests, and choosing the right varieties of fruits and vegetables to grow, among other topics. The goal is to make gardening a relaxing and enjoyable experience.

When planning the design and layout of your garden, browse on Pinterest, social media, and magazines for inspiration.

Where Do I Start?

So, you want to grow your own food and create your own vegetable garden? Don't worry too much about the small nitty-gritties just yet. Remember: Getting started is half the battle won!

1 Find Inspiration.

The first step to planning your garden is to get inspired and to visualize your dream garden. Browse through gardening books and magazines, search on Pinterest, Instagram, YouTube, and other social media channels for inspiration, and make note of the garden styles and landscape colors that move you. Once you have a collection of inspiring photos or a mood board, find the commonality between them. Do you gravitate toward raised beds or in-ground gardens? Do you like the look of formal, structured gardens or a billowing country-side meadow? Are you attracted to soft, muted colors like pinks, peaches, and lilacs, or do you prefer vibrant hues like yellow, orange, and red? Understanding your style and preferred aesthetics will guide you when it's time to actually build your dream garden.

2 Observe Your Space.

Another important consideration before building your garden is to understand the practical limitations of your space. Take a walk through your proposed garden area. Observe and find the sunniest spot. Locate the closest water source or spout. Look for slopes and indentations in the landscape. Are there any animals or critters (such as deer, rabbits, chipmunks, etc.) that frequent

Before you install your garden, observe your space for sunlight, access to water, slope, etc., and make notes.

your garden? If so, fencing might be an important consideration. Do you live in a townhouse or apartment where you can only grow in containers on a deck or patio? All these observations will help you make practical garden plans so you can grow food stress-free.

3 Know Your Frost Dates.

Knowing your first and last frost dates is crucial to gardening success. The time between your last and first frost date is often referred to as the "growing season." Warm-season crops, such as tomatoes, cucumbers, peppers, eggplants, beans, and melons, are planted on or after your last frost date and die when the weather starts getting colder and the first frost hits. Cool-season crops, such as spinach, mustards, cilantro, parsley, peas, carrots, beets, and kale and other brassicas, can survive a light to moderate frost and can be planted many weeks before your first and last frost date. Frost dates vary from region to region, depending on your location on the map. To find out the frost date for your particular area, simply search on the Internet for the term "frost date" combined with your postal code or the name of the closest major city.

Deciding What to Grow

Choosing what to grow is hands down the most fun part of gardening. Trust me, once you start browsing those glorious seed catalogs, you'll want to grow almost everything. It's really easy to go overboard when it comes to buying seeds and seedlings. Follow these tips so you can grow not just the most delicious varieties, but also the most productive ones for your climate.

1 Grow According to the Season.

Most crops can be placed into one of two categories: frost-tolerant veggies (also known as cool-season crops) and frost-sensitive veggies (known as warm-season crops). Frost-tolerant veggies, as their name suggests, thrive in the cooler temperatures of spring, fall, and even a mild to moderate winter. Surprisingly, they can handle a light to medium frost. A few examples are spinach, cilantro, parsley, carrots, beets, lettuce, brassicas like kale, cabbage, cauliflower, broccoli, and Brussels sprouts. When it gets too hot, these plants tend to bolt (go to flower) and their flavor profile changes; they usually end up tasting spicy or bitter. Warm-season crops thrive in the late spring, summer, and early fall, and they often die when temperatures go down to or below freezing. Examples of frost-sensitive veggies are tomatoes, cucumbers, peppers, eggplants, squash, melons, beans, and corn. When you grow according to the season, gardening becomes a breeze because your plants thrive. Plus, you'll get harvests that are more flavorful and abundant!

2 Grow What You Eat.

Make a list of what you and your family love to eat. You'll get the most joy out of your garden when you grow what you love. Look at your grocery receipts. What produce do you purchase most often? Tomatoes, onions, garlic, potatoes? Or maybe it's herbs, lettuce, kale, or carrots? Plan to grow what you know your family will eat. Now take it a step further by adding to the list a few items that you've never tried before and would like to experiment with. Perhaps that list includes plants like ground cherries, cucamelons, or soybeans/edamame? Always grow one or two varieties that are new to you—that's what keeps gardening fun and interesting! At the end of the day, don't waste time growing something that you won't enjoy eating. You'll quickly realize that garden real estate is quite precious. So, grow what you love and eat what you grow!

A colorful harvest from my late spring garden.

Grow according to the season. Tomatoes, basil, cucumbers, and peppers are just some of the crops you can grow easily in summer.

3 Choose Award-Winning Varieties.

Success in the garden not only depends on soil health, but on variety selection as well. Choose varieties that are labeled "bush," "patio," "pickling," "dwarf," or "cherry." These varieties are often the most prolific while requiring less space in the garden. Also, select varieties that have a good disease resistance. Lastly, when in doubt, go for award-winning varieties. All-America Selections (AAS) is a nonprofit organization that selects top-performing varieties in different categories of edible plants and vegetables each year and lists their top performers on their website. Other countries may have their own awards program for fruits and veggies, such as The Royal Horticultural Society's Award of Garden Merit (AGM) in the UK, for example. Be on the lookout for regional winners wherever you live.

Selecting the Right Location

Choosing the right spot for a vegetable garden is often the most confusing and overwhelming part for most gardeners. It really doesn't have to be. Follow these simple tips to find the best location for your garden or to make the most of the landscape that you've got.

1 Observe Your Landscape.

I want you to spend some time walking and observing the landscape of your home/yard with intention and purpose and making notes on what you see. Which areas get the most sunlight? Is your backyard on a slope? Is it shaded by too many trees or buildings? Does water collect in particular spots of your garden after a rain? Do you find animals such as deer, rabbits, or chipmunks in your yard?

The ideal location for your garden should be based on these observations. For example, you might want to consider a front yard garden if that's the area that gets the most sunlight. If your yard is on a steep slope, you could build a beautiful terraced garden. Grow your vegetable garden on your deck, patio, or balcony so animals like deer can stay away.

2 Locate the Sunniest Spot.

Ideally, you want to situate your vegetable garden in a location that gets the maximum amount of sunlight every day. This is usually the south-facing side of your home or yard if you live in the northern hemisphere (and the opposite if you live in the southern hemisphere). Keep in mind that fruiting summer vegetables (such as tomatoes, peppers, eggplants, squash, etc.) have the maximum sunlight requirement and grow best with at least 8 to 10 hours of direct sunlight a day. Leafy greens and some herbs such as lettuce, arugula, spinach, cilantro, parsley, and mint can grow in partial shade with 4 to 6 hours of direct sunlight a day. If you live in a townhouse or apartment or if your yard is surrounded by trees and doesn't get too much sun, that's okay—work with what you've got and grow what thrives best in your conditions.

Containers are a great idea if gardening on a deck, terrace, or balcony is your only option.

My veggie garden is located on the south side of my house and receives maximum sunlight.

3   Proximity to Your Home/Kitchen.

There is an old adage that out of sight is out of mind. This holds true when it comes to a garden too. Try to situate your vegetable garden as close to your home, kitchen, or patio as possible. That way you will be most likely to visit it, use it, manage it, and enjoy it. You will especially appreciate the convenience of having your vegetable garden close by when, in the midst of cooking, you have to run out to grab some fresh ingredients that aren't stocked in your fridge.

A beautiful organic vegetable garden that my company, Hundred Tomatoes LLC, designed and installed for New Jersey client Rachel.

My own backyard garden, complete with a fenced-in border, gravel pathway, stakes, and trellises for structure and support.

Creating a Garden Design

Before you embark on designing your dream garden, always ask yourself how you can make it classic, timeless, beautiful, and practical. The first step is to grab a measuring tape, graph paper, pencil, and eraser, and measure your garden perimeter (length and width). This will become the border or framework within which your vegetable garden will reside. Draw this layout on graph paper and then go about plotting your structures within this area. Here are four elements of a gorgeous garden design.

1   Borders.

Always frame your garden's border to create a visually beautiful space and to give it structure and definition. A border can be created by laying out bricks, stones, or landscape edging around the perimeter of your garden. A border could also be a fence to prevent animals and critters from entering your garden.

2 Structures.

Structures consist of raised beds, pots/containers, fountains, trellises, composters, storage shed, potting bench, greenhouse, seating area, etc. that will be inside your garden. Decide where you want to place them and then figure out the dimensions. I usually like to place the greenhouse and composters at the back of my garden and have raised beds in the middle. You might want a fountain or birdbath in the middle of your garden, flanked by raised beds around it. Seating is best placed in areas that are shaded by trees or structures to make it comfortable and enjoyable in summer. Make sure you plot out these structures on your graph paper along with the dimensions of your raised beds or growing area. Practically speaking, I prefer my raised beds to be no more than 4 feet (1.2 m) wide so I can access it easily from all sides.

3 Pathways.

Make your garden practical by having at least 2½ feet to 3 feet (75 to 91 cm) of space between raised beds to allow for easy movement of people, bagged products, and possibly a wheelbarrow. You can leave the pathways with the existing grass or lawn if you wish, but I find that it often leads to grass creeping in and growing inside the raised beds (which calls for frequent weeding and maintenance). Instead, remove the existing grass or sod and line the bottom of the garden area with either weed barrier fabric or a layer of cardboard or carpenter's paper to suppress the weeds. To make your pathways comfortable to walk on, you can install a few inches of wood chips or gravel.

4 The Extras.

Make your garden the talk of the town with a few extra special touches. Add lighting to your garden to make it pop in the evenings and at night. Hardwired LED lights, solar lights in the corners of your raised beds, string lights, pathway lights, or lanterns will enhance the beauty of your garden and make it a magical space. Add trim on the top for seating as a finishing touch. I like to use 2-inch × 4-inch (5 cm × 10 cm) wood for sturdiness. Another way to customize your garden is by painting your raised beds with nontoxic, low VOC, food-safe paint to match the exterior of your home. Don't forget to add beautiful trellises and arches for beauty and functionality.

Creating a Planting Plan

Once you know the size and dimensions of your raised beds or planting area, the fun part begins! What will you grow? The best advice I can give you is to grow according to the season. Depending on where you live, I recommend having at least two planting plans—one for the cool season (cold-hardy veggies that can tolerate a frost) and one for the warm season (heat-loving crops that die when frost hits). There are three different ways in which you can plant your raised beds.

1   Monoculture Method.

In this method, each bed is planted with one single crop. For example, all cabbages are planted in one bed, tomatoes are planted in one bed, peppers are planted together, etc. This works especially well in traditional farming in order to speed up sowing and harvesting for economies of scale. When growing this way, it is essential to follow crop rotation practices in order to reduce pest pressure and have a healthy harvest each year. The disadvantage of this method is that if a particular pest attacks one plant, then the entire family of plants can succumb to damage.

2   Polyculture Method of Using Thrillers, Fillers, and Spillers.

For most home gardeners, an ideal way of planting a garden would be to mix it up using the polyculture method. Here each bed is planted with a variety of crops from different plant families, so pests get confused. This is also the founding principle of companion planting. Mixing a variety of plants creates show-stoppingly beautiful and productive vegetable gardens! If you choose to grow different crops together, then follow the classic "Thriller, Filler, and Spiller" philosophy to know what to plant where.

Tall plants or "thrillers" should be planted in the center of your garden, raised beds, or containers. These are tall statement veggies that add height and drama to your garden. A few examples are corn, sunflowers, wheat, tomatoes, okra, and dinosaur kale. Climbing plants such as cucumbers, pole beans, and peas also fall in this category if they are supported vertically on a trellis.

Plant "spillers" on the edges or corners for an element of softness and whimsy. These are plants that trail and spill over. Examples include sweet potatoes, strawberries, trailing nasturtiums, prostrate rosemary, oregano, thyme, petunias, melons, pumpkins, etc.

Grow "fillers" in between the thrillers and spillers. These should be medium-sized plants and act almost like ground cover, hiding the soil. Good examples are peppers, eggplants, basil, marigolds, zinnias, carrots, beets, Swiss chard, kale, cabbage, lettuce, spinach, arugula, radishes, and herbs like cilantro, parsley, sage, and dill.

3 Intensive Planting or Square Foot Gardening Method.

Lastly, maximize your growing space and minimize weeds by planting intensively. Of course, you don't want to overcrowd the garden because then the seedlings will remain stunted as they compete with each other for nutrition. A good rule of thumb is to look up or visualize what a large, grown plant will look like and allocate proper space accordingly. When in doubt, follow Mel Bartholomew's square foot gardening method, which tells you the number of plants to grow per square foot.

My intensively planted vegetable garden, growing everything from tomatoes, kale, ground cherries, squash, and more.

Here's a sample summer planting plan for my client. It follows the polyculture method of planting a variety of crops in raised beds.

How to Build a Classic Raised Bed

I love gardening in raised beds—they're easy on the back and aesthetically pleasing, and after filling them with good soil and plants, you're ready to go. In this chapter I'll teach you how to build a classic raised bed that's 4 feet × 4 feet (1.2 m × 1.2 m) in dimension and 10 inches (25 cm) tall. It's deep enough to grow root vegetables like carrots and plants with a deep root system like tomatoes too. An added bonus is that it has a convenient ledge to sit on as you lean in to harvest. Here's how to build your own classic raised bed that will last for 7 to 10 years.

MATERIALS NEEDED

For Sides of Raised Bed

Long Boards: Two pieces of 2" × 10" × 48" (5 cm × 25 cm × 122 cm) untreated Cedar or Douglas Fir Wood

Short Boards: Two pieces of 2" × 10" × 45" (5 cm × 25 cm × 114 cm) untreated Cedar or Douglas Fir Wood

For Top Trim or Ledge of Raised Bed

Trim Boards: Four pieces of 2" × 4" × 50" (5 cm × 10 cm × 127 cm) untreated Cedar or Douglas Fir Wood

Other Materials

24 pieces of Multipurpose Screws #10 × 2½"

8 pieces of Trim Head Screws 3⅛"

Drill and Drill Bits

Miter Saw

Measuring Tape

Pencil

Rubber Mallet

Sanding Paper

Strap Clamp

Framing Square

Wood Glue

Safety Glasses

Gloves

Leveler

Step 1: For making the sides of the raised bed, I recommend purchasing two pieces of wood in the following dimension: 2" × 10" × 8' (5 cm × 25 cm × 2.5 m). Cut one board in half so you end up with two long boards that are each 48" (122 cm) in length, and cut the other board so you end up with two shorter boards that are each 45" (114 cm) in length. Think of the raised bed from an aerial perspective. The reason why the wood boards are cut to different lengths is because when you purchase wood, store labels will say that it's 2" (5 cm) thick. However, the actual thickness is usually 1½" (4 cm). Measure to check your wood; you may need to saw off twice the thickness of your wood to create two short boards. Hence, you will be left with two long boards and two short boards.

Step 2: For the top trim, take the 2" × 4" × 50" (5 cm × 10 cm × 127 cm) wood boards, and using a miter saw, cut the edges at a 45-degree angle.

Step 3: To assemble the raised bed, attach the two short boards to the insides of the long board using a drill and multipurpose screws. You can make a pilot hole first and then drill twelve multipurpose screws (three on each side—one on the top, one in the middle, and one at the bottom). Use a framing square to make sure the corners are straight.

Step 1: Cut the wood to size so you have 2 long boards, 2 short boards, and 4 trim pieces.

Step 2: Cut the trim at a 45-degree angle using a miter saw.

Step 3: Attach the short boards to the insides of the long board.

Step 4: Use a strap clamp to help attach the last long board to make the raised bed.

Step 5: Glue trim together.

Step 4: When attaching the last long board, either have someone help you hold it in place, or use a strap clamp. Use a rubber mallet to ensure that the wooden boards are all level and straight.

Step 5: To build the top trim, add some wood glue to the mitered edges and stick the trim boards together in place. Use the strap clamp to hold the glued trim pieces tightly so they stick. Measure the corners with a framing square to ensure that they are flush and straight.

Step 6: Secure the trim together (don't just depend on the wood glue to hold it in place) by drilling eight of the trim head screws at the corners, two on each side.

Step 6: Secure the trim by drilling trim head screws at the corners.

Step 7: Attach the trim on top of the raised bed by using multipurpose screws.

Step 7: Don't forget to drill a multipurpose screw in the middle of the trim to attach it to the raised bed.

Classic 4' × 4' (1.2 m × 1.2 m) raised bed that's 10" (25 cm) tall is ready for gardening.

Step 7: Attach the trim to the top of the raised beds (I place mine in the middle, so that there's a slight overhang on both sides—inside and outside). Use the remaining twelve multipurpose screws and drill them on the top of the trim to secure it to the raised bed side. Use two screws on each corner and one screw in the middle.

Finishing Touches

Before you place your raised bed in the garden, you can sand it down for a smooth finish. For critter protection, staple hardware cloth to the bottom. You can also stain your raised bed with a nontoxic, food-safe waterproofer stain or rub linseed oil for longevity. Before adding soil to your raised beds, line the bottom with a layer of cardboard to suppress weeds and then add good quality organic soil and lastly organic plants and you're all set to grow!

Finishing touches like a nontoxic, food-safe stain and lighting can elevate the look of a garden. Featured here is my client Rachel's garden.

Line the bottom of your raised beds with cardboard or weed barrier fabric before filling with soil.

Filling raised beds for my client Jocelyn Dannenbaum with my special soil blend recipe (mentioned on page 25).

How to Fill Raised Beds

SOIL CALCULATOR

In Cubic Feet

Multiply:
length × width × height

In Cubic Yards

Divide:
length × width × height / 27

For example, a raised bed that is 8' long, 4' wide, and 1' tall will need: 8 × 4 × 1 = 32 cubic feet of soil or 32/27 = 1.19 cubic yards of soil

If 1 bag of soil has 2 cubic feet of soil, Then you will need 32/2 = 16 bags of soil

If there's one place in the garden where you should focus the majority of your energy on, it's the soil. Good soil is the foundation of a healthy, thriving, and productive garden. Make sure you nurture the soil and soil biology with good gardening practices, such as regular application of compost, leaving roots intact in the ground to break down and feed soil life over winter, and planting cover crops in fall to add back nitrogen and minerals that may have been depleted over the growing season.

When it comes to filling your raised beds, there are many options to choose from, but before you do, I highly recommend lining the bottom with layers of flattened-out cardboard (earthworms love it, plus it suppresses weeds). Here are three ways to fill your raised beds.

1 Bagged Organic Potting Soil.

Buying bagged organic soil from your local nursery or gardening center makes sense when you have a few raised beds or containers to fill. A good rule of thumb is to buy soil that is specifically made for organic vegetable gardening and raised beds. Read the ingredients list and make sure it contains lots of diverse and rich organic matter, such as earthworm castings, compost, poultry manure, bat guano, kelp meal, alfalfa meal, feather meal, mycorrhizal fungi, biochar, greensand, etc. You can always buy some of these amendments individually and add to your soil as needed. You also want your soil to have ingredients that help with aeration, water retention, and drainage, such as coco coir, perlite, and vermiculite.

2 My Secret Recipe.

When you have several raised beds that you need to fill, buying bagged soil products can quickly become expensive. It's always a good idea to call your local stone yard, gardening center, or co-op and order soil and compost in bulk. Fill your beds with a blend of 30 percent topsoil (filler material), 30 percent compost (organic matter), 10 percent vermiculite (for water retention), and 5 percent perlite (for drainage). Add these ingredients to the raised beds and mix. As a last step, add in the remaining 25 percent that comprises organic bagged potting soil meant for raised beds and vegetable gardens. Don't mix it in with the rest of the materials; simply add it on top as a final layer into which seedlings will be planted.

3 Hugelkultur Method.

This is a classic method of filling very tall raised beds, where the bottom gets filled with logs of wood, twigs, and branches and then a layer of grass clippings goes on top, followed by unfinished compost or topsoil and finally adding good quality potting soil or bagged vegetable garden soil on the top 6 to 8 inches (15 to 20 cm), followed by mulch. Please note that this method works best when your raised beds are over 1½ to 2 feet (46 to 61 cm) tall. Another thing that you need to be careful about is that if you add too much woody materials at the bottom, it can deplete your beds of nitrogen (key nutrient for leafy growth in plants) as the logs of wood, twigs, and branches pull nitrogen from the soil in order to break down over time. Ideally, let your hugelkultur-style raised beds settle down for several months before planting in them.

Irrigating the Garden

Water is the lifeblood of a garden. There are many ways to water your garden, from using a simple watering can to installing sophisticated drip irrigation. Decide how you plan to water your plants before you build your garden. First, locate the nearest water source or spigot connection and make sure that the garden isn't located too far away from it. Next, choose from one of these great irrigation options.

1   Drip Irrigation.

Investing in a drip irrigation system is an excellent idea for those who have busy lives, love to travel, or don't have time to water their garden. Apart from convenience, one of the main reasons why I love drip irrigation is because it waters the plants at soil level thus keeping the leaves and foliage dry (greatly reducing the chance for disease and pests). If the thought of installing your own irrigation system intimidates you, call your local landscaping company or irrigationist and ask them to install it for you. Companies such as Rain Bird, DripWorks, and Garden in Minutes offer great drip irrigation options. Most of these systems are so advanced that they can be controlled with an app on your phone. Some even have advanced weather sensors to detect rainfall (and automatically adjust watering accordingly) and most come with several years of warranty too.

2   Hand Watering and Oyas.

A small garden can be easily managed by hand watering using a watering can or a hose pipe with a nozzle that has different functions. I also like installing oyas or ollas (clay pots with a long neck that are filled with water and buried under the soil). They release water through osmosis and can be a great tool in dry, hot summer months. When hand watering, make sure that you water as close to the soil level as possible to avoid soil from splashing back on to the leaves and causing disease.

Hand watering using a watering can is the simplest way to water the garden.

Burying a clay olla under the soil. This is a wonderful option for watering your garden in the hot, dry summer months.

3 Rainwater Harvesting.

The benefits of rainwater in the garden are numerous. For one, it's free! Two, it's higher in nitrogen when compared to municipal or well water, and three, it's eco-friendly as it reduces the depletion of groundwater. To capture and store rainwater, all you need is a rain barrel that is connected to your rain gutters. Fit it with proper filters to strain out the debris, and make sure it is closed properly so it doesn't become a breeding ground for mosquitoes. Before using rainwater that has been collected using this system in your vegetable garden, it may be a good idea to get a sample of the collected water tested to make sure there are no chemicals or bacteria like *E. coli* present. Empty out your barrel in winter if you experience a freeze.

What Are the Easiest Crops to Grow?

RESH RECOMMENDS: Easy-to-Grow Varieties

If you're a beginner gardener and don't know where to start, then use this list as a guide for crops that are easy to grow—that will give you a win in the garden and will motivate you to want to grow even more next year!

- ☐ 'Sungold' Cherry Tomato
- ☐ 'San Marzano' Tomato
- ☐ 'Homemade Pickles' Cucumber
- ☐ 'Beit Alpha' Cucumber
- ☐ 'Hansel' Eggplant
- ☐ 'Fordhook' Zucchini
- ☐ 'Shishito' Pepper
- ☐ 'Olympus' Bell Pepper
- ☐ 'Genovese' Basil
- ☐ 'Santo' Cilantro

- ☐ 'Bright Lights' Swiss Chard
- ☐ Blue Curled Scotch Kale
- ☐ 'Red Cored Chantenay' Carrots
- ☐ Sugar Snap Peas
- ☐ 'Little Gem' Lettuce
- ☐ 'Astro' Arugula
- ☐ 'French Breakfast' Radish
- ☐ Giant Red Mustards
- ☐ 'Walla Walla' Onions
- ☐ 'Music' Garlic

1   Herbs.

Mint, basil, dill, sage, rosemary, oregano, thyme, parsley, cilantro, chives . . . the list goes on. Herbs are one of the easiest crops to grow. Most pests tend to stay away from them because of their intense fragrance, so they make wonderful companion plants too. They are easy to maintain, and the more you harvest, the bigger and bushier they will grow. Herbs are also container-friendly plants. Buy herb seedlings from your local nursery or gardening center and transplant them into the garden. Cilantro, parsley, and dill are quite cold hardy and grow best in cooler temperatures of spring and fall, while basil, rosemary, oregano, thyme, and sage thrive in summer months.

Bountiful harvest from my backyard garden.

Cherry tomatoes are very easy to grow and 'Sungold' cherry tomatoes are one of my favorite varieties.

2 Salad Greens.

Leafy greens such as a variety of different lettuces—iceberg, romaine, speckled lettuce, mizuna, endive, arugula or rocket—are not just extremely easy to grow but mature super quickly too. Baby greens can be ready to harvest in just 25 to 30 days, while whole heads of lettuce may take a little longer. Just 4 to 6 hours of sunlight is sufficient for them. They can even grow under the shade of large plants such as broccoli or tomatoes. The ideal time to grow salad greens is in the cooler months.

3 Garlic.

If you've never grown garlic before, you'll be shocked at how easy it is. The best part is that it stores very well. Yes, it does take time (almost 9 months) to go from sowing to harvest, but it's one of those crops that you plant and then forget about until it's time to harvest. Garlic is usually planted two weeks before your average first frost date, in soil that has been amended with plenty of organic matter such as compost. Separate the individual cloves (keeping the wrapper or skin intact). Plant each garlic clove 4 inches (10 cm) deep, with the pointy side facing up. Space them 4 inches (10 cm) apart in rows that are 5 inches (13 cm) apart.

4 Cherry Tomatoes.

My favorite cherry tomato varieties are 'Sungold', 'Supersweet 100', and 'Black Cherry' tomatoes. Since they are smaller in size, you will find that cherry tomato plants are not just more prolific, but they are also early producers when compared to your regular-sized, larger tomatoes. Plant them deep and stake them well. These can easily grow 6 to 8 feet (1.8 to 2.4 m) tall, so they do need a good amount of support.

Preventing Weeds

Why is it important to prevent weeds in your vegetable garden? It's not because they are unsightly—it's because weeds can spread rapidly and deplete the garden soil of nutrition. This means that while weeds will thrive and grow, your fruit and vegetable plants will be hungry for more. Here are some great ways to prevent and reduce weeds in your garden.

1   Cardboard or Carpenter's Paper.

Before installing soil and compost in your raised beds or in-ground garden, line the bottom with one to two layers of cardboard to help suppress weeds. You can do this by saving the boxes from your online shopping, removing the plastic tape and labels, and flattening them out like you would on recycling day. Make sure that you overlap the cardboard pieces to avoid any gaps or holes where weeds can grow through. Once you lay down the cardboard, add your soil on top. The layers of cardboard block out sunlight and effectively kill the weeds below. You can use carpenter's paper as a substitute for cardboard. The benefits of using cardboard is that it's a biodegradable material and earthworms love to feed on it, which in-turn adds back more nutrients to the soil (through earthworm castings).

2   Weed Barrier Cloth or Landscape Fabric.

Another option to suppress weeds is to use weed barrier cloth (also known as landscape fabric) as an alternative to cardboard. The advantage is that it's more durable and can last up to a decade when compared to cardboard, which typically breaks down within 8 to 12 months. When installing weed barrier fabric, make sure that the fabric overlaps each other at the edges to prevent weeds from poking through. Secure to the ground with landscape staples/pins.

3   Wood Chips.

Mulching your garden pathways with wood chips is a great way to reduce weeds in your garden. Wood chips are made by chopping up parts of trees such as branches, trunk, and bark into smaller bits. When installing wood chips, I highly suggest that you clear the grass or sod from the area, add layers of cardboard, and then add wood chips on top. Wood chips will eventually break down and add organic matter back into the soil. Contact your local tree removal company to source wood chips for your garden.

Gravel suppresses weeds, looks aesthetically pleasing, and is easy to walk on too.

Clockwise from top right: Wood chips, gravel, carpenter's paper, weed barrier fabric, and cardboard.

4 Gravel.

Another popular and aesthetically pleasing way to suppress weeds is to use gravel on the pathways of your vegetable garden. Level the area first and install weed barrier fabric prior to installing the gravel. Gravel is easier to walk on when compared to wood chips, it facilitates good drainage, and the best part is that it comes in a variety of shapes, sizes, and colors to complement the look of your home.

Hardware cloth is reinforced on top of welded wire mesh to create a fence that will deter squirrels and chipmunks.

Custom fencing to prevent deer and critters from entering the veggie garden of my client Rachel's garden.

Protecting the Garden from Deer and Critters

You can spend a lot of money on building your dream garden, but if deer, chipmunks, voles, and other critters come visiting, digging up seedlings, eating all your veggies, and destroying the garden, all your hard work will be futile. Here are some of the best, tried, true, and tested options for keeping deer and critters away from your vegetable garden.

1   Fencing.

Yes, fencing can be an expensive proposition, but it is the only method that can truly keep deer and critters out of your garden. Fencing can be made out of many different materials and what you select can depend on your budget and aesthetics. Some great options are prefabricated vinyl fencing, wooden fencing, or DIY/custom fencing using 4-inch × 4-inch (10 cm × 10 cm) wooden posts pushed into the ground every 6 feet (1.8 m) apart and wrapped with welded wire mesh (that is 1½-inch × 1½-inch or 4 cm × 4 cm in diameter or smaller). T-posts can also be used as an alternative to wooden posts.

Ideally, fencing should be 8 feet (2.4 m) tall so deer can't jump over it. When installing fencing, tightly wrap welded wire mesh around the entire fence, stapling it to the wood fence posts (or securing it with zip ties to the t-posts). For extra protection, reinforce the bottom 3 or 4 feet (91 or 122 cm) of the fence with hardware cloth. This will deter rats, chipmunks, and squirrels from climbing in as they will be afraid that their legs might get stuck in the small holes. Make sure that you dig a trench at least 12 inches (30 cm) under the ground when installing fencing and bury the hardware cloth underneath too so that digging animals, such as voles and rats, can't get in.

Electric fencing and motion-activated sprinklers work well, especially for deer, but you need to be careful about turning them off when you're entering the garden and especially if you have little children.

2 Hardware Cloth.

Hardware cloth is a very versatile material to use in the garden. Not only can you use it to reinforce fencing to prevent animals from coming in, but you could also staple hardware cloth on the bottom of your raised beds to prevent digging animals, such as rats, voles, and gophers, from getting in from the bottom. Another great way to use hardware cloth is to lay it flat on top of your soil after direct sowing seeds. Little seedlings can easily grow through the open holes, but animals will avoid walking over the hardware cloth to dig up your seeds.

3 Cloches or Covers.

If fencing isn't in your budget, then use cloches, insect netting secured with landscape staples, chicken wire wrapped around the base or trunk of individual plants or fruit trees, and even cover seedlings with clear plastic bins to prevent them from being chewed up. Don't be afraid to get creative and do it yourself.

I grew this lettuce seedling under grow lights in my basement. The plant looks healthy and not at all root bound.

Chapter 2

STARTING FROM SEED

G rowing your own food from seed can be one of the most satisfying and reward-ing experiences in your gardening journey. It not only allows you to save a lot of money on buying transplants from nurseries, but it also gives you the freedom to grow and enjoy new varieties that you may never have tried before.

The first decision you need to make when sowing seeds is whether you should start them indoors or directly sow them outside in the garden. If you live in a cold climate where you experience frost, snow, and below freezing temperatures, and have a short growing season (the time between your last and first frost dates), then sowing seeds indoors can give you a head start to an earlier harvest. Direct sowing seeds outside in the garden is recommended for root crops and legumes, such as carrots, radishes, beets, parsnips, peas, and beans.

When it comes to indoor seed starting, timing is everything. Start something too early and the plant can become root bound in its little container. Start too late and you won't be able to enjoy the harvest from your crop due to insufficient growing time.

Starting from seed is as simple as pushing a seed into some soil, watering it, giving it sufficient light, and watching it grow. In this chapter, I will help you navigate and troubleshoot common seed starting mistakes and problems. From choosing the right seeds, soil mix, containers, and grow lights, to recognizing problems and fixing them in simple, easy ways.

To make your task simple, I have created a Seed-Sowing Guide so you know what to grow and when to grow it. All you need to know is your first and last average frost dates. Find that out by searching on the internet for "Frost date for your postal code."

SEED-SOWING GUIDE

	15 wks	14 wks	13 wks	12 wks	11 wks	10 wks	09 wks	08 wks	07 wks	06 wks	05 wks	04 wks	03 wks	02 wks	01 wks	Last Frost	01 wks	0
Vegetables																	before / after	
Arugula				SI	SI	SI	SI	TR	TR	TR								
Artichoke				SI	SI	SI	SI	SI									TR	
Beets (DS)												DS	DS	DS				
Bok Choy						SI	SI	SI	SI	TR	TR	TR						
Broccoli								SI	SI	SI		TR	TR	TR				
Cabbage						SI	SI	SI	SI	SI	TR	TR	TR	TR				
Cardoon								SI	SI	SI							TR	
Carrot (DS)											DS	DS	DS					
Cauliflower								SI	SI	SI	TR	TR	TR	TR				
Celery					SI	SI	SI										TR	TR
Collards				SI	SI	SI				TR	TR							
Corn (DS)																	DS	DS
Cucumber												SI	SI	SI			TR	T
Eggplant								SI	SI	SI								T
Ground Cherry								SI	SI	SI								T
Kale						SI	SI	SI		TR	TR	TR						
Kohlrabi						SI	SI	SI				TR						
Leeks				SI	SI	SI						TR	TR	TR				
Lettuce						SI	SI	SI				TR	TR					
Melons														SI	SI			T
Mustards						SI	SI	SI			TR	TR						
Okra												SI	SI	SI	SI		SI	T
Onions		SI	SI	SI							TR	TR						
Peas (DS)				SI	SI	SI	SI	TR	TR	TR								
Peppers								SI	SI	SI								T
Pumpkins														SI	SI			T
Quinoa								SI	SI	SI						TR	TR	T
Radish (DS)										DS	DS	DS						
Spinach (DS)									DS	DS	DS	DS						

SI Sow seeds indoors   TR Transplant seedlings outside   DS Direct sow

	15 wks	14 wks	13 wks	12 wks	11 wks	10 wks	09 wks	08 wks	07 wks	06 wks	05 wks	04 wks	03 wks	02 wks	01 wks	Last Frost	01 wks	02 wks
												before					after	
Squash														SI	SI	TR	TR	
Swiss Chard								SI	SI	SI								
Tomatoes								SI	SI	SI	SI						TR	TR
Watermelon														SI	SI			TR
Herbs																		
Basil											SI						TR	
Dill					SI	SI	SI								TR	TR		
Eucalyptus			SI	SI	SI											TR		
Lemon Balm								SI	SI	SI		TR	TR					
Oregano		SI	SI	SI		TR	TR	TR	TR	TR								
Parsley			SI	SI	SI						TR	TR	TR	TR				
Rosemary		SI	SI	SI	SI	TR	TR	TR	TR	TR								
Sage								SI	SI	SI				TR	TR			
Stevia								SI	SI	SI							TR	
Thyme			SI	SI	SI	SI	SI										TR	
Flowers																		
Amaranth								SI	SI	SI							TR	TR
Borage (DS)														DS	DS			
Calendula								SI	SI	SI							TR	
Chamomile								SI	SI	SI							TR	
Cosmos (DS)																	DS	DS
Dahlia											SI	SI					TR	TR
Dianthus		SI	SI	SI										TR	TR			
Echinacea						SI	SI	SI						TR	TR	TR		
Marigold				SI	SI	SI	SI	SI									TR	TR
Nasturtium (DS)														DS				
Pansy		SI	SI	SI										TR	TR			
Petunia						SI	SI	SI									TR	
Sunflower (DS)																	DS	DS
Strawflower								SI	SI	SI							TR	
Zinnia												SI	SI				TR	

What Type of Seeds Should I Buy?

When it comes to growing from seed, people are often confused about the difference between heirloom, hybrid, open-pollinated, organic, and non-GMO seeds. It's important to know the different types of seeds that are available in the market and to choose the right ones that align with your goals as a gardener.

1   Open-Pollinated.

If seed saving is your goal, then it's important to buy seed varieties that are open-pollinated. Open-pollinated seeds come from plants that have pollinated naturally, either by self-pollination or by cross pollination (via wind, birds, bees, insects) with another plant of not just the same species, but also the same variety. When you buy seeds that are open pollinated, it means that you will be able to grow a crop that will genetically be very similar to the parent plant or "true to type."

2   Heirloom Seeds.

All heirloom seeds are always open pollinated. What classifies a variety as an heirloom is the amount of time that they have been passed down over generations. If an open-pollinated seed variety has existed for more than 50 years, it's usually considered an heirloom. Most heirloom seeds have great interesting stories attached to them and date back hundreds of years. When people migrated and moved from one place to another, they often took their beloved seeds with them to grow and enjoy the same flavors as their ancestors did.

Lots of gardeners love growing heirloom varieties because of their incredible flavor, history, cultural significance of where they came from, and of course for seed saving too.

3   Hybrid Seeds.

Hybrid seeds are created by crossing two different varieties of the same species. This is usually done to create a stronger plant that has the best traits of both parent plants, such as disease resistance, flavor, yield, vigor, etc. Such plants will have a label called F1 hybrid. If seeds are saved from the F1 hybrid plant, they are called F2 hybrid. Avoid saving seeds from hybrid plants as you will not get consistent results.

Just so you know, hybrid seeds that are sold to home gardeners are not genetically modified in a lab and are not GMO seeds. Hybridization can and often does occur in nature too, when the pollen from two different varieties creates a new variety all together.

'Dr. Wyche's Yellow' heirloom tomato grown from seed. One of my absolute favorites!

I grew all this food from seeds, a combination of heirloom and hybrid varieties.

Depending on your goals as a gardener, it might be wise to include both open-pollinated and hybrid varieties in your vegetable garden so you get the best of both worlds—flavor and history from heirlooms and yield and disease resistance from hybrids.

4   Organic Seeds.

Seeds that are considered organic are saved from plants that have been grown organically for at least three years using certified organic gardening practices and not sprayed with artificial chemicals or pesticides. Just because a seed is open pollinated, heirloom, or hybrid does not mean that it is organic.

5   GMO Seeds.

Currently, the US, UK, and India are just some of the countries that do not allow for the sale of genetically modified seeds to home gardeners. However, in the US, certain crops grown for commercial purposes can use GMO seeds—such crops are corn, sugar beets, soybeans, and canola. Many companies that do not buy or sell genetically engineered seeds and plants have signed the Safe Seed Pledge.

The Best Growing Medium for Indoor Seed Starting

Did you know that you can start seeds in a medium completely devoid of soil? Seeds need a light and fluffy growing medium so that their roots and shoots can grow easily without much resistance. Below are a few great options to use for a seed starting medium. I'll tell you all about their pros and cons and how to supercharge your seed starting mix for success.

1   Bagged Organic Seed Starting Mix.

If you're a beginner gardener, or starting just a few trays of seedlings, buying a bag of organic seed starting mix from your local gardening center or a big box retailer makes the most sense. When selecting a mix, please read the ingredient list at the back of the package, which would include peat moss or coco coir, perlite, and/or vermiculite. Some seed starting blends include additional ingredients such as mycorrhizal fungi and earthworm castings, which provide gentle nutrition to the seedlings but aren't essential for the actual germination process.

The advantage of buying bagged mixes is that they are ready to use and take the guesswork out of the process. The disadvantage is that they can be expensive.

2   DIY Seed Starting Mix.

The big advantage of making your own seed starting mix is that you can save money when buying ingredients in bulk. Here's my recipe:

5 parts peat moss or coco coir   ½ part fine perlite
1 part fine vermiculite   ½ part earthworm castings

Mix the ingredients together until you have a homogenous mixture.

3   Peat Pellets or Compressed Coconut Coir Discs.

If you're a first-time gardener and want to grow from seed, using peat pellets or compressed coco coir discs makes it very easy. All you have to do is add water and they will expand. They have a fine mesh netting on the outside, which allows for airflow and water absorption and prevents the growing medium from disintegrating. Once the discs enlarge, simply poke a small hole on the top and plant your seeds.

Seed Starting Mix Ingredients

Peat Moss	Peat moss is decomposed organic matter that looks just like soil and is a sterile growing medium that is slightly acidic in nature. It helps with water drainage and prevents compaction. It is extracted from the earth by draining peat bogs, which are essential for sequestering carbon from our environment. The process of harvesting peat releases CO_2 into the atmosphere. It can take millennia to replace these bogs; hence, peat moss is considered a nonrenewable resource.
Coco Coir	Coconut coir is a by-product of the coconut fiber industry. It is essentially the outer husk of the coconut shell. Considered a sustainable alternative to peat moss. The husk is often soaked in saltwater or freshwater to loosen the fibers. Salt in the fibers can stunt plant growth, so wash/rinse before use. Mostly sourced from India and Southeast Asia, coco coir can leave a higher carbon footprint when you consider the transportation cost to the US or rest of the world.
Perlite	Perlite is made of lightweight volcanic glass and helps with water drainage.
Vermiculite	Vermiculite is a granular mica-based mineral that helps with soil aeration and water retention.

What Kind of Containers Should I Use?

Once your seed starting mix is ready, it's time to put them into containers. With so many options to choose from, something as simple as selecting a pot/container can feel overwhelming. Not to worry, I'm listing my favorite options, to make the choice super easy for you.

1 Solo Cups.

This is my personal favorite container when it comes to indoor seed starting. Solo cups are not only inexpensive, but they are also easily available everywhere, including at grocery stores, and their size is perfect for seedlings both large (tomatoes) and small (lettuces). Clean them, store them, and reuse them again and again. Another advantage is that you most likely won't need to pot-up your seedlings into larger containers and risk disturbing their roots.

Before adding your seed starting mix into solo cups, make sure that you poke holes at the bottom for drainage.

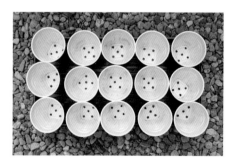

Solo cups with holes drilled at the bottom are my favorite seed starting container. I clean and reuse them year after year.

Seventy-two cell seed starting trays are ideal for germination, but you will need to transplant or prick out seedlings rather quickly to prevent them from getting root bound or stunted.

2 Yogurt Containers.

Large 32-ounce (900 g) yogurt containers are amazing for seed starting bigger plants that grow very fast, such as cucumbers and squash. They are also perfect for potting up seedlings (like tomatoes) that have outgrown their seed cells or solo cups. The lids make a perfect tray for catching excess water that may drain out of the container (saving your table/carpet/furniture in the process) and they also double up as a humidity dome to facilitate germination when seeds have just been sown.

3 Seed Cells.

Seed cells, seed trays, plug flats—these all are different names for one and the same thing: seed starting containers. They come in a variety of sizes and configurations—from six cell packs, thirty-two cell packs, seventy-two cells, and so on. These are fine for basic germination. However, you will need to transplant, pot-up, or prick-out seedlings from these small cells once the cotyledons (first set of leaves) or true leaves (second set of leaves) have erupted.

The advantage of growing in seed trays that have a large number of cells is that you can save a substantial amount of money on seed starting mix versus filling up solo cups or large yogurt containers only to find out that the seeds didn't germinate. Having smaller trays also makes the seed starting process quicker and more manageable in the beginning. The disadvantage is that you need to be a bit more skilled at transplanting seedlings from these cells.

4 Biodegradable Pots or Paper Pots.

Many people think using biodegradable containers or even empty egg cartons are a great alternative to using plastic products. While that might be true, their porous material tends to make moisture evaporate very rapidly, which means plants get thirsty quite often and you have to water frequently. This cycle of frequent watering ends up disintegrating the pots quite easily and often leads to fungal issues as well. Use them if you wish for starting seedlings that grow quickly and can be transplanted into the garden soon.

Choosing the Best Grow Lights

If you want success with indoor seed starting, then using grow lights is a must. Without them, your seedlings will be weak and leggy as they stretch for light. So many different types of grow lights are available today that deciding which one to buy can be confusing and overwhelming. Here's a breakdown of what you should look for when choosing to buy grow lights.

1 Fluorescent Lights.

Fluorescent lights are an affordable and effective option for seed starting. These are easily available at big box retailers and you can choose to use T5 or T8 bulbs. T5 bulbs are thinner, brighter and have a higher lumen output compared to T8 bulbs. They are also more energy efficient, yet more expensive than T8.

2 LED Lights.

You might have seen red- and blue-colored grow lights used in seed starting. These are LED lights and they are great for indoor gardening. Blue light helps with leafy, vegetative growth while red light is great for flowering and fruiting. Some LED lights also emit white light, which is a combination of different colored lights in the spectrum. LED lights are considered more energy efficient and are a great choice for indoor seed starting, yet they are more expensive than fluorescent bulbs.

3 Full Spectrum Grow Lights.

A grow light is considered full spectrum when it most closely resembles daylight and emits red, blue, ultraviolet, and infrared lights as well. Both fluorescent and LED lights can be full spectrum.

4 Color and Kelvin.

Kelvin represents the color temperature of a light and can range from 1,000 (red/warm light) to 10,000 (blue/cool light). For healthy plant growth, choose a grow light that has a Kelvin value of 5,000 K to 6,500 K (K stands for Kelvin).

Full spectrum grow lights being used for indoor seed starting.

Some LED grow lights emit both blue and red lights. Blue light helps with vegetative growth, while red light helps with flowering and fruiting.

5 Brightness and Lumens.

Another factor to consider when purchasing grow lights is its brightness, which is measured in lumens. Brighter lights with higher lumens can be placed further away from the top of the plants, while grow lights with lower lumens (like 2,500 to 5,000 lumens) need to be closer to the top of the seedlings (2 to 3 inches or 5 cm to 8 cm away). You can increase the lumens or increase the brightness by adding more bulbs or grow lights over your seedlings. The advantage of having a grow light with higher lumens is that light can shine on a wider area or canopy and seedlings growing on the edges or sides get the same amount of light as the ones in the middle

Why Haven't My Seeds Germinated?

It's happened to the best of us—we've sown the seeds, invested in the best setup, and patiently waited for our seeds to sprout. But time goes by and nothing happens! As a gardener, we know that timing is everything, so when seeds fail to germinate, it can be a really frustrating experience. Below, I've listed the most common reasons why seeds fail to germinate and what you can do proactively to avoid this problem.

1   Poor Viability of Seeds.

Seeds can last a really, really long time if stored and cared for properly. Yes, seeds can and do expire and their viability does go down with time. When you sow seed from an old seed packet you will notice a lower germination rate. This means that it may be time to buy a new seed packet so you can have dependable results. To make your seeds last a long time, store them in a cool, dark, and dry place. I know many people swear by storing their seeds in the refrigerator. If you don't have fridge space, then a suitable area of your house or basement will work just fine. Please avoid leaving your seed packets out in the sun and definitely don't leave them out in the rain. To increase their longevity, store your seeds/seed packets in an airtight container. I personally love using photo boxes or vintage recipe boxes for storing my seeds.

2   Sowing Seeds Too Deep.

Avoid sowing seeds too deeply into the seed starting mix. A seed only has a little energy stored inside it to help it germinate. So, if the seed is sown too deep, it may never end up reaching the top of the pot of soil.

You won't believe how shallow most seeds like to be planted! The general rule of thumb is to sow the seed as deep as twice the width of the seed. The bigger the seed, the deeper it goes. Use a toothpick or pencil to make a little dent in the seed starting mix, where the seeds will be planted and then cover them ever so lightly with soil. I generally recommend sowing two to three seeds per cell or container to increase the chances of success—if one doesn't germinate, you'll have another to rely on.

Avoid spotty germination of seeds by sowing at least 2 to 3 seeds per container.

Seeds can last several years, but their viability goes down with time. Write down the date when you received the seeds on top of the seed packets.

3 Dry Soil.

The most common reason for seeds not germinating is letting the soil dry out or sowing seeds in a seed starting mix that is too dry to begin with. Moisture is absolutely crucial for successful germination. When seeds absorb water, they swell up, and it's a cue for new growth to burst out. I highly encourage you to premoisten your seed starting mix before sowing seeds. How do you know if your seed starting mix is moist enough? Do a squeeze test. When you squeeze your premoistened mix, it should form a nice firm ball in your hands and a little water should drip out and run off between your fingers. The ball of soil should stay firm when you open your fist but should easily disintegrate if you touch and push it gently.

Make sure that the seed starting medium is loose and fluffy so roots can grow easily. Heavy, compacted soil often leads to stunted seedlings.

Why Are My Seedlings Stunted?

Very often seedlings germinate just fine, but then suddenly stop growing taller and stay stunted. This is usually a plant's way of telling us that it is experiencing stress of some sort. Unfortunately, once a seedling is stunted, it's hard for it to recover, grow tall, and be healthy and productive. Here are a few common reasons why seedlings can become stunted. Knowledge is power, and once you learn what can cause this problem, it's very unlikely that you will let that happen to your plants.

1   Seed Starting Medium Is Too Heavy and Compacted.

Don't try to grow your plants indoors in the same way that they are grown outside—in potting mix, garden soil, or a medium that's too heavy, compacted, or has lots of sticks and stones in it. Remember, seeds need a light, fluffy, and fine textured growing medium so their roots can grow easily. When the medium is too compact-ed, two things can happen: One, roots have to push very hard to grow, and two, a compacted/heavy medium prevents air from reaching the roots and essentially suffocates them. This can cause a seedling to become stunted and sometimes rot and die altogether. Avoid this problem by using ingredients such as perlite to fluff up the soil and help with drainage. If your growing medium has a lot of sticks and stones in it, sift it out by using a sieve. Sometimes adding too much worm castingsor organic matter in your seed starting mix can make it heavy too—make sure that it's no more than 5 percent to 10 percent of your mix.

Overcrowding and not thinning out seedlings often leads to stunted growth as each seedling is unable to receive the nutrients it needs to grow.

2 Overcrowding Seedlings.

Don't wait too long to thin out your seedlings. Too many seedlings growing in one container is a recipe for disaster. They will compete with each other for nutrients and get stressed and stunted because they don't have enough room to grow. I recommend separating, pricking out, or thinning seedlings once the true leaves (second set of leaves) have formed. This will give them sufficient space to grow and thrive. Use a pair of scissors to snip off extra seedlings or separate them carefully and transfer them into their own individual container. See the section on separating seedlings on page 60.

3 Leaving Them in the Pot for Too Long.

The most common reason for stunted seedlings is leaving them in a small container or seed starting cell for too long. Plants grow at a shockingly fast speed and seedlings can get root bound very quickly if the container is too small to keep up with their growth. Lift up your seed tray or container from time to time and look at the roots peeking out from the bottom. Observe the leafy growth on top. If you think a plant seems too large for its container, you're probably right. Pot up the plant into a larger container to give it room to grow.

Grow healthy seedlings by placing grow lights close to your plants.

Preventing Leggy Seedlings

Grow healthy seedlings by placing grow lights close to your plants. If your seedlings look tall, thin, and lanky instead of being thick and stocky, it's probably because they desperately need more light and are stretching tall in search of it. Most beginner gardeners, excited about growing from seed, place their seedlings on a sunny windowsill with the best of intentions. Most seeds don't need light to germinate, but once the newly sprouted seedlings start peeking out from the soil, they do need 14 to 16 hours of light to grow and thrive. Supplemental lighting works wonders when it comes to indoor seed starting.

1 Turn the Lights on Immediately upon Germination.

The moment your seeds germinate, remove the humidity dome or any cover you may have, take the tray off the heat mat, and place the seedlings directly under grow lights. How far you place your seedlings from the light will depend on the type of lights you use. Fluorescent shop lights with 3,000 to 5,000 lumens should be placed 2 to 4 inches (5 to 10 cm) away, while high intensity LED lights with higher lumens should be placed further away, so as to not burn the leaves. Read the instruction manual that comes with your grow lights, observe the growth of your plants, and adjust the distance accordingly. One of the most common mistakes is having your lights suspended too far away from the seedlings. If it's hard for you to move your grow lights up and down, prop up your seedlings on top of a stack of books, boxes, or bins to elevate them closer to the light source.

2 Keep the Lights on for 24 to 48 Hours after Germination.

You may have noticed that not all your seeds germinate at the exact same time, though most germinate within 1 to 2 days of each other. This is why leaving grow lights on for the first 24 to 48 hours straight, without turning them off, is a good idea. This allows the majority of the plants to benefit from being exposed to light immediately upon germination. This is especially important if you're growing in seed cells or modular trays, and you can't move individual germinated seedlings under the grow lights.

3 Mimic the Wind.

To create strong, stocky seedlings with thick stems, use an oscillating fan near your seedlings. The gentle wind from the fan mimics the wind in nature and provides the needed resistance to make the seedlings strong and healthy. Good air circulation also helps with overall plant health. Place the fans on the same timer as your grow lights. Use a cycle of 14 to 16 hours on and 8 to 10 hours off. I know many people suggest leaving the fans on for 24 hours a day, which is fine too, but it may dry out the soil very quickly. Also, did you know that running your hands gently over the top of your seedlings works wonders as well? It creates a slight resistance, which makes plant stems stronger.

Yellowing leaves in seedlings are often a sign of nutritional deficiency. Fertilize with half strength of organic liquid fertilizer, such as earthworm casting tea or fish emulsion, twice a month.

Yellowing leaves are a common occurrence in seedlings that have been overwatered or underwatered as roots are stressed and unable to transport sufficient nutrition to the rest of the plants.

Why Are My Seedlings Turning Yellow?

Yellowing seedlings are a very common occurrence and nothing to fret about as it's a problem that can be easily fixed. As with everything, catch the problem early to give your seedling the best chance of survival.

1 Nutrient Deficiency.

The most common cause for yellowing seedlings is nutritional deficiency. Most store-bought seed starting mixes are completely devoid of nutrients. Even those that list some nutrients on the package have it in very small amounts so as not to burn the roots of tender seedlings. Besides, keep in mind that seed starting pots or containers fit a very small amount of seed starting mix in them, so nutrients get depleted quite fast, especially as the plant grows bigger and bigger.

To counteract this problem, it's important to start fertilizing seedlings once they are 2 weeks old. Use an organic liquid fertilizer bimonthly. You can increase it to a weekly application once seedlings are larger in size. While choosing a liquid fertilizer, select one that's high in nitrogen, which helps with leafy green growth in plants. I recommend using something as gentle as earthworm casting tea or fish emulsion at half strength (follow package directions). Keep in mind that fertilizing won't turn yellow leaves green. However, it will ensure that new leafy growth is lush, green, and healthy. Organic liquid fertilizers can create a distinctive smell in your seed starting area, but rest assured your plants will definitely love it.

2 Overwatering or Underwatering.

As gardeners we have all been guilty of overwatering and underwatering our plants at some point or the other. Overwatering seedlings suffocates the roots and they cannot deliver essential nutrients to the plant. This causes yellowing leaves. Underwatering creates the same phenomenon as water is the channel by which plants transport nutrients from the roots to the different parts of the plant. Watering the right amount at the right time does not need to be rocket science. In fact, you can easily know that it's time to water your seedlings by simply picking up the container/pot or seed tray with the seedling in it. If it feels lightweight and the top of the soil looks dry, then please go ahead and water your seedlings. If it's heavy and the soil looks moist, then you can wait longer before watering.

3 Root Bound.

Yellowing leaves in seedlings can also be a sign that the plant is root bound and that it has outgrown its small container. To determine if the seedling is root bound or not, pick up the seedling and check the bottom of the container. If you find lots of roots sticking out of the drainage holes, it could mean that the plant is stressed and needs more room to grow. Remedy this situation by transplanting or potting up the seedling into a larger sized container.

Preventing Fungus Gnats

When growing seedlings indoors, sometimes you might find pesky, small, black flying insects that look like fruit flies hovering around your seedlings or sitting on top of the leaves and soil. These insects are called fungus gnats. They reproduce very rapidly, and if they are not controlled, they can wreak havoc on your plants! Your seedlings will display symptoms such as wilting, yellowing, and overall poor growth. If you want healthy plants, then it's important to get rid of fungus gnats. Here's how.

Yellow sticky traps are very effective at attracting fungus gnats.

1   Yellow Sticky Traps.

Yellow sticky traps work really well in attracting and getting rid of fungus gnats without the need to use any chemicals on your seedlings. Most sticky traps are attached to little sticks and part of the stick is pushed into the soil in your seedling container, sort of like a flag. The bright yellow color attracts the gnats—they get stuck to it and eventually die. These traps can easily be purchased online or at your local gardening center.

2   Oscillating Fan.

Another great option to deter fungus gnats is to use an oscillating fan near your seedlings. The wind from the fan will prevent the gnats from coming close to the seedlings. Air circulation from the fan tends to dry out the soil, which in this case is a good thing because soil that is constantly wet or damp is what attracts and harbors fungus gnats in the first place. Of course, you don't want your soil to dry out to the point that it hurts your plants, but you definitely don't want to overwater your indoor seedlings.

Let the seed starting mix cool down to room temperature and then add the seeds.

3 Adding Hot Water to Seed Starting Mix.

Very often fungus gnat eggs can hide inside packaged seed starting mixes, which may have been sitting on shelves for several months—or even years! Gnat eggs are notorious for staying dormant in dry soil and they come to life and start breeding in moist soil. You can kill fungus gnat eggs by adding boiling hot water to moisten your seed starting mix. Before you add the hot water, read the ingredients and make sure that your seed starting mix is completely devoid of nutrients and beneficial microbes as you don't want to kill the beneficials in any way. After adding the hot water, let your seed starting mix cool down to room temperature and then add worm castings, AZOMITE, mycorrhizae fungi, and other amendments to supercharge your seed starting mix.

Sowing Small/Tiny Seeds

The problem with sowing small seeds is that you can invariably end up sprinkling a lot more than just two to three seeds per cell, which not only wastes a lot of seeds but also requires extra seedlings to be snipped off or thinned out. Overcrowded seedlings leads to competition for nutrients and often leads to poor health and growth and can result in stunted seedlings. To prevent these problems from happening, here are a few tips and tricks to help you sow small seeds with ease.

1   Toothpick Trick.

To sow really small seeds, all you will need is a toothpick and a little bowl of water. Pour out some tiny seeds from your seed packet into a shallow dish. Fill your seed trays or containers with premoistened seed starting mix and follow the instructions below:

Step 1: Dip the blunt end of the toothpick in the bowl of water.

Step 2: Use the blunt, wet end of the toothpick to pick up one or two seeds that are sprinkled on the shallow dish. You will notice that one seed will immediately get attracted to the toothpick and stick to it almost like a magnet.

Step 3: Transfer the seed from the toothpick into the premoistened seed starting mix by dipping the wet toothpick with the seed into the soil. Repeat the process with more seeds as needed.

While this simple toothpick trick might sound time consuming, it gets easy with practice. However, if you have a very large number of tiny seeds to sow, this may be impractical for you.

2   Try Pelleted Seeds.

Pelleted seeds are tiny seeds that are coated, usually with organic clay, to make them uniform and larger in size and hence easier to handle. Their larger size also makes it easier for gardeners to use with mechanical seeding tools. I often use pelleted seeds for carrots and lettuce.

3   Premoisten Your Seed Starting Mix.

The best tip I can give you when it comes to sowing small or tiny seeds is to premoisten your seed starting mix so you don't need to water after sowing. If you sow small seeds and then water on top of them, you will end up dislodging the seeds or burying them even deeper, which can lead to spotty germination.

Once you master this toothpick trick to sow tiny seeds, you'll wonder why you never tried it before! All you need are seeds, a toothpick, a little bowl of water, and a container with soil.

Step 1: Dip the blunt end of the toothpick in water.

Step 2: Touch the seed with the wet tooth-pick and the seed will stick to it immediately and easily.

Step 3: Place the small seed into the soil by brushing the toothpick against the soil. You're done!

4   Cover with Vermiculite.

Did you know that small seeds barely need to be covered with soil? The general rule of thumb is to sow seeds twice as deep as their width. When seeds are tiny, that can be very hard to do. But here's a solution—once you sow a few seeds on top of your premoistened seed starting mix, cover them with a light sprinkling of vermiculite instead of more seed starting mix. Vermiculite is very light in weight and hence seeds can sprout very easily with that medium on top. It's especially helpful when sowing basil and lettuce seeds.

The plants in my organic backyard garden are quite literally powered by earthworm castings and earthworm castings tea, which provides gentle nutrition and never burns the roots.

Fertilizing Seedlings

Most seed starting mixes are practically devoid of nutrition and those that do have some amendments don't have enough to support a seedling for the full 6 to 8 weeks of indoor life. Also keep in mind that the seedlings are growing in small containers and their roots do not have access to sufficient soil and nutrients like a plant would in nature. This is why supplementing with fertilizers becomes important. There are plenty of great organic fertilizers available; however, one word of caution: Seedlings are small and fragile, so dilute your fertilizers and use them at half strength. Also, use an organic liquid fertilizer or a water-soluble liquid fertilizer because plants can absorb it immediately.

1   When to Fertilize Seedlings.

Once seedlings have germinated success-fully and the cotyledons (first set of leaves) and true leaves (second set of leaves) have emerged, it's time to think about nourishing the seedlings over the next few weeks until they are ready to be set out into the garden. I recommend fertilizing seedlings once they are about 3 inches (8 cm) tall or approximately after they are 2 weeks old. This is because the seed itself has enough stored energy to germinate and produce true leaves, but after that, a seedling depends on you to provide it with the nutrients it needs to grow strong and healthy.

The ideal time to start fertilizing seedlings is when their true leaves (second set of leaves) have formed.

2   How to Fertilize.

My favorite natural, organic liquid fertilizer for seedlings (and plants too) is earthworm casting tea, also known as worm tea, vermicompost tea, or compost tea. It is made via a process that involves soaking worm castings (poop from earthworms) in water. The resulting liquid or "tea" is high in nutrients, superb and gentle for fertilizing seedlings. It won't burn the roots of your plants and adds beneficial bacteria that creates a great environment for encouraging growth. Another organic option is to use fish emulsion or liquid seaweed or kelp, again at half strength of whatever is recommended on the package directions. All these options can be a bit smelly, but when diluted and used, you won't notice too much.

3   How Often to Fertilize.

When plants are small, start by fertilizing them once every 2 weeks. As they get larger, you can switch to fertilizing them weekly. Also observe your plant. If leaves are yellowing, it might indicate that they need more nutrients too. Having a consis-tent fertilizing routine makes a big difference.

Use a pencil or a fork to prick out and separate seedlings. Push down at an angle and then in an upward motion, popping out the seedling.

Once the seedling has been pricked out, transplant it into its own individual container. Avoid holding the seedling by its delicate stem.

Separating Seedlings

As a gardener, it's a wonderful feeling to see seedlings pop up after sowing seeds not too long ago. More seedlings means more plants of course, but make sure that you don't leave them sitting together in one cell or container for too long. Seedlings need space to grow and thrive and don't like competing with one another for nutrients and resources.

There are many easy ways to thin out or separate seedlings, but you need to time it correctly. In this case, sooner is usually better than later. Here are your options.

Vegetable Gardening Made Easy

1   Scissors to Snip Off.

Many beginner gardeners might find the task of separating multiple seedlings to be daunting. Even experienced ones might say that they don't have the time for it. Thinning seedlings by simply snipping off extra ones with a pair of scissors is often the easiest way out. Cut off the weakest seedlings at the base, close to soil level, and leave the healthiest or biggest one to grow.

As a gardener, I can attest to the fact that snipping off extra seedlings is indeed a painful process as each little seedling represents a potential healthy plant and bountiful future harvest. If the thought of snipping off extra seedlings bothers you, then read on for tips on how to separate seedlings instead.

2   Pencil/Fork Trick to Prick Out.

If you don't want to snip off excess seedlings, here's an easy hack to separate seedlings using a pencil or a fork. Push the pencil/fork deep into the soil at an angle and gently move it upward to pop out the seedling. Holding the seedling by the leaves, transplant it into its own individual container. This trick works best when seedlings are still quite small and no more than the true leaves (second set of leaves) have grown. Don't forget to add a label so you know the variety.

3   Tease Apart.

Seedlings that are larger in size can be tricker to separate as roots often get tangled up together in the pot. You might have noticed seedlings sold in nurseries and gardening centers often have several growing together in one cell. Don't worry, plants are quite resilient and a bit of damage to their roots won't hurt them too much, but like I mentioned before, the sooner you separate them, the better. The way to tease seedlings apart is to pop them out of the container and gently pull all the seedlings out, soil and all. Then using a gentle back and forth motion, tease apart the roots as much as possible. Don't worry if the soil or seed starting mix falls away at this point. Transplant the seedlings into their own individual containers that have been filled with either screened potting soil or seed starting mix blended with some earthworm castings for nutrition.

Whichever way you choose to separate the seedlings, make sure you water them after they have been potted up into their new home or container.

Tips to Harden-Off Seedlings

Hardening-off seedlings is exactly what it sounds like—toughening them up by slowly introducing them to their natural environment to get them ready for their life in the garden.

While growing indoors, seedlings have been sheltered from harsh elements like wind, rain, extreme temperature fluctuations, and pests. If seedlings are not hardened off properly, their leaves can get burned from exposure to natural sunlight; they can fall over easily from wind and rain and undergo what's known as transplant shock. Many gardeners (myself included) have lost seedlings to transplant shock. Hardening off seedlings by transporting them in and out is quite possibly the most tedious task of indoor seed starting, but one that is absolutely necessary. You're now in the home stretch.

Below are the dos and don'ts on how to properly harden off your seedlings.

1   Do start the hardening-off process at least 1 to 2 weeks before seedlings are ready to go into the ground. The reason that the timeframe is approximate and not exact is because sometimes weather conditions in your area, such as a rainstorm, a windy day, and extreme hot or cold temperatures, might prevent you from moving the seedlings outdoors for hardening off. It's better to err on the side of caution than let months of hard work and preparation go to waste.

2   Do check the weather forecast before you place your seedlings outside. Ideally, choose a warm, cloudy day when temperatures are over 50°F or 10°C. This is especially important for hardening off warm weather crops, such as tomatoes, cucumbers, eggplants, peppers, squash, etc., which can suffer if temperatures get too cold.

3   Do harden off your seedlings by placing them under a shaded area, such as a covered patio, on the first few days. Exposing them immediately to direct sunlight will likely cause scalding, discoloration, and wilting.

4   Do place seedlings outside in late afternoon or early evening when the sun's rays aren't too harsh. Gradually increase the amount of time you leave the seedlings outside, usually an extra hour or two per day.

5   Do place your seedlings in trays so transporting them in and out becomes easy.

6   Do check your seedling soil for moisture. Outdoor elements such as wind and sun can dry out the soil quite quickly, leaving your plants thirsty for more.

My seedlings are getting hardened off outside on a cloudy day.

Start the hardening-off process by placing your seedlings in a shaded location first. Exposing them to too much direct sunlight can result in sunburn on the leaves as seen in this photo.

7   Don't harden off your seedlings in the middle of the afternoon. Bright midday sun will cause the leaves to scald, burn, and wilt.

8   Don't forget to bring your seedlings back inside at night. I highly recommend setting an alarm on your phone to help you remember. On the last 2 days, seedlings can be left outside overnight too.

9   Don't leave your seedlings outside on a very rainy or windy day, nor on a very hot or cold day. Seedlings will simply suffer and many gardeners have lost seedlings this way.

10 Don't worry if your seedlings get a little sun scalding or sunburn. As long as fresh new growth looks green and healthy, the plant will be fine.

Beautiful summer harvest of organic food, grown from seed in my garden.

Chapter 3

HOW TO GROW FOOD & MAXIMIZE PRODUCTION

N ow that you've learned how to start your own plants indoors from seed, let the fun part begin—growing, harvesting, and enjoying your fresh, homegrown food! You will probably agree with me that nothing tastes better than food that you've grown yourself. With food prices going up every year, it's no surprise that more and more people are taking to gardening and growing their own fruits and vegetables.

This chapter is going to be all about maximizing food production from your garden. You will also learn tips and tricks to help you grow the maximum amount of food possible with minimum effort. I will also teach you how to troubleshoot gardening problems, such as getting your green tomatoes to turn red, getting hot peppers to become spicy, preventing your lettuce from tasting bitter, and making sure you grow straight carrots every time.

And who doesn't want to achieve the best results with minimal cost or investment? Learn all about mulching your garden to conserve water, using grocery store produce such as sweet potatoes and scallions to grow food for free, and propagating and multiplying plants such as tomatoes, basil, and more to grow an endless supply of food.

Once you know some of these basic gardening techniques such as hand pollination, pruning, propagation, and spacing, you can apply them to many different crops and achieve the same great results again and again each year.

Finally, I want you to keep one thing in mind: Real homegrown food won't always look perfect, but it will taste incredible, be nutritious, and bring you immense joy and satisfaction in knowing that you grew it yourself.

Cheers to growing more!

Lettuce is one of those crops that can either be directly sown in the ground or transplanted. Ideally, transplant lettuce seedlings in spring and direct sow lettuce seeds in fall.

What Crops Should I Direct Sow vs. Transplant?

Should you sow seeds directly in the garden or transplant seedlings instead? If you live in a cold climate with a short growing season, transplanting seedlings after your last frost date will most definitely give you a head start and enable you to harvest fruits and vegetables sooner than if you had directly sown seeds instead. But direct sowing too has its place in the garden, especially for those plants that don't like their roots being disturbed (which can often happen during the transplanting process). Here's a list of crops that benefit from direct sowing.

1 Root Vegetables.

Root veggies such as carrots, radishes, beets, turnips, and parsnips benefit a great deal from direct sowing seeds into the ground. This is because these plants are grown for their roots itself and disturbing the tap root by transplanting seedlings will more likely than not create a root vegetable that looks deformed, has a weird shape, or does not grow at all. That isn't to say that you absolutely cannot transplant root vegetables. You can. Just the likelihood of success will be lower.

2 Beans and Legumes.

Other vegetables that dislike being transplanted are legumes, such as peas and beans (bush beans, pole beans, long beans, runner beans, lima beans, fava beans, garbanzo beans, soybeans, just to name a few). Their roots are quite sensitive and dislike being moved. Beans are quick to sprout; however, peas (which are often sown in the cooler months of early spring) take longer to germinate. To facilitate germination in peas, soak them overnight in some water. Drain out the excess water and sow the seeds in the ground. Soaking peas helps soften the outer coat of the seed and that's what enables/ speeds up germination.

Peas, beans, legumes, and root veggies like carrots, radishes, and beets should ideally be directly sown in the ground.

3 Plants with Large Seeds.

There are many crops with substantially larger seeds that can also be direct sown in the garden. This is because large seeds are easier to handle, they germinate quickly, and you don't have to worry about caring for seedlings indoors. A few examples of such crops are cucumbers, zucchini, pumpkin, butternut squash, okra, melons, and corn.

4 Fall Grown Veggies.

When planting my fall/winter garden, I often direct sow seeds in late summer/early fall. The soil is nice and warm, which facilitates germination. Quick-maturing varieties, such as lettuce, bok choy, mustards, radishes, cilantro, and parsley, are ideal for direct sowing. Veggies that take 90 to 100 days to grow and mature, such as broccoli, cabbage, cauliflower, and Brussels sprouts, are usually planted as transplants. This strategy helps me maximize my garden space and gets me timely harvests.

Top to Bottom: Some of my favorite ingredients that I add to supercharge the soil or planting holes before transplanting seedlings are mycorrhizal fungi, slow-release granular fertilizer, and earthworm castings.

Freshly transplanted seedlings in my client Cara Silman's kitchen garden include everything from peppers, eggplants, cucumbers, cherry tomatoes, marigolds, and a variety of herbs. Don't forget to add plant tags or labels.

Transplanting Seedlings

The day is finally here! The sun is shining, you're excited to get your hands in the dirt and get your veggie garden all planted!

When to Transplant

If you're transplanting your warm-season crops (tomatoes, peppers, eggplant, cucumbers, squash, melons, etc.), make sure that the chance of frost has passed and temperatures are consistently over 50°F or 10°C. Ideally, you want to select a cloudy day to transplant your seedlings so that the heat and light from the sun doesn't stress them out.

If you're looking to transplant cold-hardy seedlings into your spring garden (brassicas, spinach, peas, parsley, cilantro, mustards, lettuce, arugula, etc.), then you can plant most seedlings 4 to 6 weeks before your last frost date and once the ground is workable (meaning, not hard and frozen). Keep emergency covers, such as frost cloth or plastic bins, on hand to cover seedlings in case of an unexpected snow storm or cold snap.

How to Transplant

Step 1: Create a good foundation for your seedlings by amending or refreshing the soil. Add 3 to 4 inches (8 to 10 cm) of compost on top of your existing soil. If compost isn't available, add good quality bagged garden soil that's high in organic matter, such as worm castings, kelp meal, feather meal, composted manure, just to name a few.

Step 2: Water your seedlings before transplanting them so the process can be as stress-free for them as possible.

Step 3: Dig the planting hole. For small seedlings such as lettuce, a dibber should work well. Larger seedlings such as tomatoes need a deeper planting hole and a hand trowel is ideal.

Step 4: Add additional nutrients into the planting hole, such as earthworm castings, a handful of all-purpose granular fertilizer, and AZOMITE, to provide micro and macro nutrition for your seedling. Gently scratch/mix the ingredients into the planting hole.

Step 5: Remove the seedling from its container by turning it upside down and gently squeezing the sides of the container.

Step 6: Sprinkle mycorrhizal fungi to the root area of the seedling. This will help the roots create an association with the soil and make the plant grow stronger.

Step 7: If your seedling is very root bound, don't be afraid to tease apart or gently tear some roots from the bottom.

Step 8: Finally, transplant your seedling into the planting hole, backfill with soil, and don't forget to add the label.

Step 9: If your plant is a tall, vining, or climbing variety (ex: peas, cucumber, indeterminate tomato, pole beans, loofa, etc.), then make sure you install a trellis, stake, or plant support at the time of transplanting. Doing it later might mean disturbing or tearing into established roots.

Step 10: Finally, give your plants a nice deep watering and you're all set.

Now watch your plant babies grow and thrive and enjoy their bounty!

Straw is excellent for mulching your garden. Here I'm using shredded straw on my raised beds.

Apply a layer of straw that is about 1" to 2" (2.5 to 5 cm) thick. If the straw breaks down over time, reapply as needed.

Using Mulch

Many people are afraid of mulching their garden because they feel it creates a hiding spot for pests, that mulch may contain weed seeds, or that it looks unattractive. Used the right way, mulch can actually reduce the spread of diseases, suppress weeds, retain moisture in the soil, insulate and protect the soil, and add organic matter as it breaks down over time. It can quickly become a gardener's best friend.

1 Types of Mulch.

There are a variety of options when it comes to mulching your garden—straw, compost, grass clippings, newspaper, dried leaves, just to name a few. I'm personally a big fan of straw, compost, and dried leaves as mulch.

When using straw, make sure that you use clean straw from a reputable source and not hay, which can have weed seeds in it. You can even buy triple shredded straw, which is smaller, finer, and breaks down faster.

When it comes to compost, you can use mushroom compost, homemade compost, or leaf compost, which provide nutrients to the plants. I like to alternate between different types of compost in my garden each year because each has its own benefits and adds a variety of nutrients, which is important for the overall health of the garden and ecosystem.

Dried leaves are another great option and can be found in abundance, especially in autumn. Use a leaf shredder if possible to chop them into finer bits and apply as mulch around your fall/winter plants. Dried leaves can be applied in fall when you put your garden to bed for winter. They can insulate and keep the soil warm in the cold winter months, add organic matter back into the soil, and feed soil biology.

Grass clippings work well too, but you need to make sure that you add a very light layer (1 inch or 2.5 cm); otherwise, it can turn into a thick, smelly, and slimy mess. Please make sure that the grass you use hasn't been sprayed with any chemicals, as you definitely don't want that in your vegetable garden.

Using newspaper as mulch sounds good, but it breaks down too quickly and I'm a bit weary of the chemicals in the inks/dyes.

2 How to Use.

STRAW:

- Apply a 1 to 2 inch thick (2.5 to 5 cm) layer of straw on top of the soil and around the base of the plant. Do not mix it in with the soil and avoid touching the stem, especially for young seedlings.

- If you are directly sowing seeds, then push aside the mulch and plant directly into the soil. Once seeds germinate and seedlings are 4 inches (10 cm) tall, then you can mulch around the seedling.

COMPOST:

- Apply compost to the garden in fall after removing spent summer plants and clearing the debris and diseased plant material from the soil. A layer of 2 to 3 inches (5 to 8 cm) works best.

- I use mushroom compost as a mulch around fall/winter plants, such as garlic, carrots, and brassicas. The layer of compost will insulate and protect the soil from freezing and protect and nourish your cold-weather plants.

3 What to Avoid.

Avoid using wood chips on top of your garden soil as they are high in carbon and can rob the soil of nitrogen as it breaks down. Instead, use wood chips to mulch your pathways and keep them weed free.

How to Prune Plants

Pruning means removal of foliage, branches, buds, and flowers to maintain the health of the plants, increase growth and production, and control the spread of diseases in the garden. Although there are many different pruning techniques, I will focus on the most common ones useful to all gardeners and that can be applied to almost any plant in your vegetable garden.

1 Rule of Thirds.

If you're looking to grow a healthy plant, it's essential to remove the bottom leaves so they don't have any contact with the soil. This prevents the spread of soil-borne diseases. Removing bottom leaves also helps maintain good airflow and keeps humidity low. I usually recommend pruning lower leaves at the time of planting (especially for tomato plants) or once the seedling has at least four sets of leaves. Whenever you're removing foliage from your plants, follow the Rule of Thirds—do not remove more than one-third of the leaves on your plant! Remember, leaves are energy factories for your plants, so don't overdo it.

2 Start at the Bottom.

When pruning leaves, I recommend starting from the bottom most leaves. This is because as plants grow bigger, new growth on top often shades out the leaves underneath and they turn yellow, brown, and dull in appearance. Bottom leaves are often not able to photosynthesize properly, and limp, dying foliage can attract pests. If you see yellowing, browning leaves at the bottom of your plants (especially kale, bok choy, lettuce, and even tomatoes, peppers, and squash), prune and discard them.

3 Deadheading.

When it comes to flowers in your garden, make sure that you regularly remove dead, dried, or dying flowers. Not only will this improve the appearance of your plant, but most importantly, it will help the plant focus its energy on producing new growth, which means more flowers for you.

4 Pinching.

Many of you might have heard or seen gardeners "pinch off" or "top off" their pepper, basil, and herb plants, which means cutting off the main stem of the plant when it's 6 to 8 inches (15 to 20 cm) tall in order to produce more side shoots. This method can work wonders, especially for herbs and flowers like basil, sage, rosemary, marigolds, etc. and creates a robust, bushy plant.

Make sure to regularly remove yellowing, browning, and diseased leaves to keep plants as healthy as possible.

Here I'm pruning the bottom leaves of a zucchini plant to encourage airflow. When pruning plants, start by removing leaves from the bottom and work your way up.

It works well for peppers too; however, one word of caution: Following this practice for pepper plants should depend on the length of your growing season. If you're in zone 6 or colder, then topping off your pepper plants may not be the best strategy as you may not have enough time left in your growing season for new shoots to form and produce flowers and fruits.

5 Cleaning Tools.

Pruning etiquette 101: Thou shall clean and sanitize tools after using them to prune plants. Simply wash your pruners or tools with dish soap and water, wipe them dry, and then dip the blades in some rubbing alcohol (containing 70 percent isopropyl alcohol) and wipe it dry. This really helps control the spread of disease in your garden.

Should I Remove Tomato Suckers?

First, what exactly are tomato suckers? Suckers are the new growth between the main stem and a side branch, sort of in the node or armpit of the plant. Suckers can grow quite large and produce their own leaves, branches, and fruits (i.e., more tomatoes for you).

It's a myth that you have to remove suckers from your tomato plants. Most gardeners recommended it, but it's really up to you.

A few years ago, I decided to let my tomato plants grow freely without removing all the suckers and quite literally grew a tomato jungle. I had to crawl underneath the plants to harvest tomatoes! It was wild and unmanageable, but the harvest was truly amazing! By late summer the tomato plants fizzled out with blight and disease and I had to pull out my plants two months before my first frost date. Which wasn't necessarily a bad thing, because I got a bountiful harvest and was able to plant my fall garden in a timely fashion.

So, what should you do—remove suckers or not? It's your choice, but here's my verdict: I suggest removing some of the suckers from tomato plants but not all of them. This allows you to have a happy medium between a manageable, healthy plant and a good harvest.

When Should You Remove Suckers?

1   If It's an Indeterminate Tomato Variety.

There are two types of tomato plants—determinate and indeterminate. Like their names suggest, determinate tomato plants grow to a determined size (compact and bushy) and will produce all their tomatoes quickly in a short, determined period of time. Removing suckers from such plants will greatly reduce your harvests, so do not remove suckers from determinate tomato plants.

Indeterminate tomato plants grow a little bit of fruit throughout the growing season, until the first frost kills them. They can grow exceptionally tall (mine once grew over 8 feet or 2.4 meters tall). If suckers are not removed, especially in the beginning of the season and on the lower branches, the plant can become very wild and unmanageable, often flopping over, branches bending or snapping off, and cages leaning with the weight of the plant. For a manageable plant, remove most suckers from indeterminate tomato varieties and make sure you stake and support your plants properly.

2 If You Want a Healthier Plant.

If you don't remove the suckers, you can quickly end up with a tomato jungle (like I did). Nothing wrong with that, but your plants will be more susceptible to blight and diseases due to lack of airflow and an excess amount of foliage.

3 If You Prefer Fewer But Larger Sized Tomatoes.

By removing suckers, the plant will not produce a large number of tomatoes, but the ones that do grow will most certainly be larger in size. This year, I regularly removed suckers from my indeterminate tomato plants and had fewer tomatoes but giant-sized ones, some weighing up to 1.7 pounds (0.75 kg).

How to Remove Suckers:

I usually prune and remove suckers from the bottom 2 feet to 3 feet (61 to 91 cm) of the plant. That way there is good airflow for the health of the plant. Ideally, remove the suckers when they just appear and are 1 to 3 inches (2.5 to 8 cm) tall. If suckers are very large, remove them carefully with pruners as you do not want to damage the main plant.

Fun Fact: Did you know that you can root tomato suckers in water and grow more plants for free? Read How to Multiply Tomato Plants for Free on page 92 to learn how to do it yourself.

Here I'm about to pinch off a small tomato sucker growing between the main stem and side branch. Removing suckers from an indeterminate tomato variety will help you manage the plant better.

There are some varieties of tomatoes that just won't turn red, such as 'Aunt Ruby's German Green', 'Dr. Wyche's Yellow', 'Cherokee Purple', 'Black Beauty', 'Sungold', and 'Black Cherry' tomato.

Why Aren't My Tomatoes Turning Red?

Every gardener I know loves to talk about the flavor of vine-ripened tomatoes. However, you might be scratching your head and wondering why the tomatoes in your garden are still green and taking forever to change color.

On average it does take 45 to 60 days from planting a seedling for a tomato to reach full maturity. But there are several factors that can affect the speed at which your tomatoes can change color from green to red.

1 Temperature.

Did you know that tomato plants are most productive when temperatures are between 68°F to 75°F (20°C to 24°C)? Yes, tomatoes thrive in warm weather; however, temperatures above 85°F to 90°F (29°C to 32°C) or below 55°F (13°C) will significantly slow down the ripening process and tomatoes will stay green on the plant for a longer period of time. If you're experiencing a heat wave or temperatures in your area have started to cool down as you're nearing autumn, tomatoes won't ripen as quickly.

To facilitate the ripening process, use a shade cloth (for heat) or fleece fabric (for cold) to protect your plants from extreme temperatures and encourage them to ripen on the vine.

2 Watering.

If you want your tomatoes to ripen or turn red quickly, then cut back a little bit on watering. This will stress the plant and encourage it to divert its energy into ripening the fruit.

3 Variety.

There are some varieties of tomatoes such as 'Green Zebra' or 'Aunt Ruby's German Green' that will remain green and never turn red. Most cherry tomato varieties will be the first to change color and ripen on the vine due to their smaller size.

Did you know that you can speed up the ripening process and turn green tomatoes red by placing them next to apples or bananas on your kitchen counter?

4 End of the Season.

As summer comes to an end and you're quickly approaching your first frost date, you will notice that tomatoes often stay green and unripe on the vine and take a long time to turn red. In this scenario, don't hesitate to harvest your unripe green tomatoes and bring them inside the house. Place them on your kitchen counter or in an empty cardboard box with a few apples or bananas next to them. The ethylene gas that is released by the fruits is scientifically proven to help speed up the ripening process in tomatoes and will turn your green tomatoes red. Flavor won't be compromised either.

A variety of spicy peppers from my garden. Top, clockwise: jalapeños, habaneros, red cayenne peppers, poblanos, and the spiciest of them all, 'Armageddon' peppers.

If you want your peppers to develop more heat, then leave them on the plant for a longer time and let them change color from green to red. Here, I'm growing spicy 'Red Rocket' chili peppers.

Why Aren't My Peppers Spicy?

Have you ever grown hot peppers like jalapeños and cayenne peppers only to taste them and find them mild and lacking in flavor? I grew the most gorgeous purple cayenne peppers this year, only to taste them and wonder where the spiciness went. I followed one of the tricks (listed at right), and by the end of the season, I grew some of the spiciest purple cayenne peppers ever!

Below are quick and easy tips to make your hot peppers taste spicy:

1 Choose the Right Variety.

Peppers get their spicy flavor from a compound called capsaicin, which creates a hot, burning sensation upon contact. The capsaicin or heat in peppers is measured on a spiciness scale called the Scoville scale. If you like hot peppers, grow ones that are higher on the Scoville scale. Some of the spiciest peppers in the world are Bhut Jolokia (ghost pepper), 'Trinidad Scorpion' pepper, 'Carolina Reaper', and 'Armageddon' pepper. If you want medium heat, then jalapeños and serrano peppers are ideal, and for mildly spicy peppers, poblanos, shishito peppers, and banana peppers are perfect.

2 Reduce Watering.

Overwatering and overfertilizing pepper plants can in fact make the peppers less spicy. Stressing the plant (just a little bit) by reducing watering once it has set fruit has been known to trigger capsaicin production in pepper plants, making the peppers more spicy. Did you know that when pepper plants are attacked by pests, they produce more capsaicin as a defense mechanism to repel them?

3 Let Fruit Ripen on the Vine.

To make your peppers spicy, don't harvest them early. Let them ripen on the vine. Peppers thrive in hot weather and the spiciness in peppers increases as the soil temperatures warm up. If you've grown peppers before, you may have noticed that all peppers often start out as green in color and then turn red and spicy when they have been allowed to stay on the plant for a prolonged period of time. This is the trick I used to turn my purple cayenne peppers spicy. I allowed them to stay on the plant and change color from green to purple to red. When I took a bite of the red-colored purple cayenne pepper, I was shocked at how spicy it was! The same happened to my shishito peppers. I missed harvesting a few of them and they ended up turning red in color and much spicier than the green ones!

Why Does My Lettuce Taste Bitter?

Homegrown lettuce is unlike anything you can ever find at the grocery store. It's sweet, crispy, fresh, and flavorful. But the first time I grew my own lettuce many years ago, it left the most unpleasant bitter taste in my mouth and I couldn't understand why. Now I know better and I'll be sharing my lettuce growing tips so you can enjoy the sweetest, best tasting lettuce ever.

1 Bolting.

Lettuce is a cold-hardy plant and thrives in the cooler months of spring and fall (and even a mild winter). It can handle a light frost too and survive freezing temperatures. Growing it in the right season makes all the difference between a sweet tasting and bitter tasting lettuce. High heat and long hours of sunlight in the summer will make the lettuce bolt (grow tall, treelike, and produce flowers and seeds). When lettuce bolts, its flavor profile changes completely and it tastes quite bitter. Once lettuce has bolted, there is no going back. Avoid this phenomenon by growing it in the right season. If you wish to grow lettuce in the summer months, choose heat-resistant varieties and/or use a shade cloth to protect your plants.

Lettuce is also one of those plants that can grow wonderfully well in the shade of other plants. I plant my lettuce seedlings in between my broccoli seedlings in spring, and when both the plants start growing, the large leaves of the broccoli plant create the perfect amount of shade for the lettuce plants to thrive. Lettuce plants (and most leafy green vegetables) can get by with just 4 to 6 hours of sunlight a day.

2 Variety Selection.

Red lettuce and speckled lettuce varieties are often more bitter tasting compared to their green counterparts. The red color comes from the presence of anthocyanins (antioxidants) in the leaves, which gives it that slightly bitter flavor. It's up to you whether you want to grow red or freckled lettuce varieties or not, but no doubt they look beautiful and are good for health.

Iceberg lettuce usually tastes the sweetest and 'Crispino' lettuce, 'Crisp Mint' lettuce, and Tennis Ball lettuce are my favorites. Buttercrunch and romaines are delicious too but not as crunchy and juicy as iceberg lettuce.

Bolted lettuce plant from my garden. Once lettuce bolts (grows tall and produces flowers), it tastes quite bitter.

The ideal time to pick lettuce and leafy greens is early in the morning. This is when they will be the most crisp and upright. Hot afternoon sun usually makes them limp and droopy.

3 Watering.

Did you know that lettuce is 95 percent water? Inadequate watering often makes lettuce taste bitter. So, water regularly and you will be rewarded with sweeter-tasting lettuce.

4 Harvest Time.

For the best-tasting lettuce, harvest early in the morning while leaves are still fresh and perky from the cool morning weather. Another tip to avoid bitter tasting lettuce is to harvest baby lettuce leaves, which have a sweet, tender taste.

Why Are My Carrots Deformed?

Growing perfectly straight carrots is almost considered the holy grail of gardening (perhaps a close second to growing tomatoes), but for some reason it eludes most people. How often have you pulled out carrots only to find them looking twisted, crooked, or like weird alien characters? Or having lush, leafy green tops with nothing underneath? Carrots are truly very easy to grow if you follow these tips below.

Spacing is everything when it comes to growing straight carrots. I follow the two finger spacing rule when thinning out my carrots, making sure that the green tops are at least two fingers apart. This has helped me grow consistently straight carrots every time.

1 Soil.

Carrots are root crops and need loose, loamy, well-draining soil. Dense, clay soil makes it hard for carrots to grow and they end up curved and deformed. Before direct sowing carrot seeds, prep your soil in the following manner:

- Fluff up the top 8 to 10 inches (20 to 25 cm) of your soil with a hand rake or cultivator.

- Amend your soil with 3 to 4 inches (8 to 10 cm) of compost or good quality bagged soil that is high in organic matter.

- Sprinkle organic fertilizer high in phosphorus, such as rock dust or bone meal, and scratch it in (follow package directions).

- If your soil is highly compacted, then mix in builder's sand or vermiculite to loosen it up. The amount that you need depends on the density of your soil.

- Make shallow trenches by lightly pressing a garden stake in the soil. Voila! Straight rows in minutes!

- Water thoroughly and deeply to premoisten the planting area.

You are now ready to direct sow some carrot seeds.

Vegetable Gardening Made Easy

Beautiful rainbow carrot harvest of 'Cosmic Purple', 'Red Cored Chantenay', and 'Amarillo' carrots.

2 Spacing.

When sowing carrot seeds, sprinkle them lightly into shallow trenches. Sprinkling too many seeds will only make it more difficult for you to thin them out later. Overcrowded carrot plants that are not properly thinned out are one of the main reasons for deformed carrots. Space rows 4 inches (10 cm) apart.

3 Thinning.

When carrots germinate and leafy greens are 15 to 18 inches (38 to 46 cm) tall, thin them out using my two-finger spacing rule: Make sure green leafy tops of carrots are spaced two fingers apart from each other and you'll grow perfectly straight carrots every time.

4 Timing.

Carrots taste best when grown in the cooler months of spring and fall. Planting carrots in summer can be tricky because the heat will make them bolt (i.e., grow lots of leafy tops, flowers, and seeds).

Did you know that carrots are cool-season plants that can handle a frost? In fact, frost converts the starches into sugar and hence fall-grown carrots taste much sweeter than those grown in spring and summer.

Why Do I Have Only Leaves and No Radishes?

Radishes are one of the fastest growing crops in a vegetable garden. They can go from seed to harvest in 25 to 30 days. They are a cool weather crop and can handle a light frost too. A very common problem that gardeners face when growing radishes is that the plants grow leafy green tops above the ground, but no root vegetables under the ground. Below you will find the most common reasons why this happens and ways to prevent it.

A harvest of my favorite 'French Breakfast' radish variety.

1 Fertilizing.

If you end up growing lots of leafy greens and no radishes at all, then the trouble might be excessive nitrogen in the soil. Radishes aren't hungry feeders like tomatoes and cucumbers. A fertilizer high in nitrogen will encourage them to put out leafy growth and not focus their energy on growing the root or actual radish. I recommend that you avoid fertilizing radish plants. If you must, then use a fertilizer that is high in phosphorus, such as rock phosphate or bone meal, which helps with root growth—which in this case is the actual radish itself.

2 Growing in Summer.

Since radishes thrive in the cooler months of spring and fall, avoid growing them in summer. Warm temperatures encourage the plant to bolt, i.e., produce flowers and go to seed, and the energy doesn't go toward producing the actual root veggie. You will also notice that radishes grown in warm weather are often spicier. So, grow them in the right season and enjoy abundant, delicious harvests.

This is what my radish patch looks like with a spacing of 1 inch (2.5 cm) between seedlings. Yes, it might look very tightly packed together, but these radish seedlings are spaced 1 inch (2.5 cm) apart from one another.

3 Overcrowding.

Just like with carrots, another common reason for growing only leaves and no radishes is incorrect spacing. At the time of sowing, space your seeds no more than 1½ to 2 inches (4 to 5 cm) apart, in rows that are 4 inches (10 cm) apart. This will allow each individual radish plant to grow properly. I also like to premoisten my soil by watering it prior to sowing seeds. If you water after direct sowing seeds, very often some seeds float away with the water and collect together in a clump, so spacing becomes a problem.

Resh's Favorite Radish Varieties

'Cherry Belle'	Easter Egg
'French Breakfast'	'Roxanne'
'Pink Beauty'	'Watermelon Radish'

A 'Galahad' determinate tomato plant loaded with fruits.

Tickle your tomato flowers to encourage pollination and ensure lots of fruit.

How to Grow Lots of Tomatoes

How often have you heard people say that there's nothing better than the taste of homegrown tomatoes? I was skeptical about it too, until I started growing my own. Growing tomatoes successfully is considered the holy grail of gardening. According to the US Department of Agriculture, each American eats approximately 22 to 25 pounds (10 to 11 kg) of tomatoes a year—that's between 75 and 100 medium-sized tomatoes! If you love tomatoes as much as I do, then here are some simple tricks to help you maximize your harvest each year.

1 Variety Selection.

If you want the most prolific tomato harvest, choose varieties that say "determinate," "bush," or "cherry" in their name or variety description. They tend to produce the highest number of tomatoes per plant, versus an heirloom tomato variety, which can produce large and delicious fruits, but the plants are less productive. Also, select varieties that are hybrids (it will say "hybrid" or "F1 hybrid" on the tag) for good disease resistance. Look for codes on plant tags and seed packets that say things like EB (resistance to early blight), LB (resistance to late blight), or F (resistance to fusarium wilt). To get a good mix of flavor and production, I like to plant a mixture of both heirloom and hybrid varieties in the garden. Here are a few examples of top-producing varieties that are my favorites: 'Celebrity', 'Galahad', 'Carbon F1', 'Sungold', 'Supersweet 100', 'San Marzano', 'Thorburn's Terra-cotta', and 'Black Cherry' tomatoes.

2 Tickle Your Tomatoes.

Did you know that an individual tomato flower has both male and female parts in it? Give the blossoms a gentle tap, shake, or tickle to release the pollen and ensure pollination (i.e., a tomato for you!). In nature, tomato plants usually get pollinated by the wind or a bumblebee, but if you want to ensure a successful harvest, give your tomato flowers a little tap the next time you head into the garden.

3 Pick Early.

Pick your first few tomatoes before they are totally ripe. This might sound crazy, but it's true. Removing the first few tomatoes while they are still a bit green and have only started blushing (changing color) stresses the plant and makes it feel like its lineage is being threatened. It sounds dramatic, but the plant then focuses its energy on producing more flowers, which in turn results in more fruits and more tomatoes for you. Try this trick when you see the first few tomatoes emerge from the plant, and you can thank me later when you have a bountiful harvest.

4 Use a Shade Cloth.

If you live in a hot climate where summer temperatures often soar above 85°F to 90°F (29°C to 32°C), you'll find that tomato blossoms tend to drop or the plant stops producing flowers. During such times—in the peak of summer—cover your plants with a shade cloth to protect them and prevent the flowers from falling off due to the heat.

Using a paintbrush, transfer the pollen from the male to the female flower.

Hand-Pollinating Cucumbers and Squash for Maximum Production

Has this happened to you: Your cucumber plant is loaded with lots of beautiful flowers, but barely any fruit? Have you gotten excited when you spotted a tiny baby cucumber, zucchini, squash, or melon form on your plant, only to find it turn soft, yellow and rot and die in a few days? This happens due to lack of pollination and there are simple ways to solve this problem and maximize your harvest.

Ideally, in nature, bees, insects, butterflies, etc. act as pollinators as they transfer the pollen from the male to female flowers when they move around the garden. However, sometimes nature can be unreliable. In such instances, what do you do? You take matters into your own hands and help facilitate the pollination process by following these steps.

1 Identify Male and Female Flowers.

Did you know that plants belonging to the cucurbit family, such as cucumber, squash, and melons, have separate male and female flowers? Female flower can be identified by an immature, small fruit at the base of the flower. Male flowers will simply have a stem and no fruit attached to it. Once you identify the male and female flowers, you can use various tools and techniques to pollinate your plants and ensure a harvest. Head into your garden and observe the flowers to identify the male and female flowers.

The first step before you hand pollinate your cucumber and squash plants is to identify the male and female flowers. Here, a female flower can be identified by an immature, small cucumber at the base of the flower. Male flowers will simply have a stem and no fruit attached to it.

2 Use a Paintbrush or Cotton-Swab to Transfer Pollen.

Using a dry paintbrush or cotton swab, gently brush it on to the anthers of a male flower, then transfer pollen onto the stigma of the female flower. And you're done! You've just successfully hand-pollinated your plant! Alternatively, you could also pluck off a healthy, fresh male flower, peel off the petals, and rub the anthers (male part containing pollen) onto the sigma of the female plant in order to transfer the pollen.

The best time to hand pollinate your cucurbit family plants is in the morning as flowers are usually fresh and open. Afternoon sun and heat can cause flowers to close or droop, which isn't ideal for hand pollination.

3 Grow Self-Pollinating Varieties.

If hand pollinating your cucumber plants isn't an option for you, then try growing self-pollinating varieties, such as 'Beit Alpha' cucumber. These are also known as parthenocarpic varieties and are ideal for greenhouse growers.

Abundant pepper harvest from my summer garden.

Shishito peppers are one of the most prolific varieties of peppers you can grow.

Growing Lots of Peppers

Since we're talking about maximizing production from your garden in this chapter, let's talk about how to grow lots of peppers in a very small space and maximize your harvest so you have plenty for pickling, canning, and sharing with friends and family. The first step to getting an abundant harvest of peppers is to start them indoors as early as 8 to 10 weeks before your last frost date so you get a head start on your growing season. Read on for more tips for an abundant pepper harvest.

1 Variety Selection.

To maximize your pepper harvest, grow varieties that are more prolific than others. Shishito peppers, jalapeños, and banana peppers are the obvious choice, but All-America Selections Winners such as 'Cornito Giallo' F1 pepper, 'Carmen' F1 pepper, and 'Giant Ristra' cayenne are super prolific as well. When it comes to bell peppers, I've found 'Gourmet' pepper, 'Olympus' bell pepper, and 'California Wonder' bell pepper to be great producers. Just keep in mind that the smaller the size of the pepper, the more prolific the plant will be.

2 Spacing.

Did you know that peppers love growing close together with their friends? Since they are a medium-sized plant and don't grow too tall, peppers are perfect for growing in containers. I like planting peppers in groups of threes in my medium sized-containers (20 inches wide × 14½ inches tall or 50 cm × 37 cm), sort of in a triangle pattern. When growing in raised beds, I plant 1 per square foot and add a stake at the time of planting to provide support.

3 Topping Off.

In order to maximize production, you want a pepper plant that's bushy and has several branches or side shoots so it can produce more flowers and fruits for you. You can encourage production of side shoots by pinching off the top of the main stem once the seedling has at least six pairs of leaves. This might seem scary and intimidating, but it totally works and makes a big difference in production. Please keep in mind that if your plant already seems bushy and has lots of side shoots, then you don't need to top off your pepper plant. Also, if you live in a cold climate with a very short summer growing season of less than 5 months, then this may not be the best strategy for you.

4 Pinching.

I encourage you to pinch off and remove all flower buds that appear on your pepper seedlings during the first 2 weeks after planting. This will encourage the plant to focus its energy on growing a strong and healthy root system versus trying to produce flowers and fruit. A stronger plant will produce more peppers for you during the growing season.

5 Fertilizing.

When your pepper plants start to put out lots of flowers, it is time to fertilize them with a fertilizer high in phosphorus (P), such as rock phosphate or bone meal, which helps with fruit production. Also be sure to sprinkle a handful of Azomite or rock dust into the planting hole at the time of planting pepper seedlings.

How to Propagate and Multiply Tomato Plants for Free

Want to grow more tomatoes but just don't have any seedlings to plant? Well, the easiest way to get more tomato plants for free (yes, you read it correctly) is by propagating suckers from existing tomato plants.

Step 1: Identify and Remove Healthy Tomato Sucker.

First step to multiplying tomato plants is to identify the sucker. What is a sucker? It is the new growth between the main stem and an existing branch, i.e., in the armpit of the plant. If you let the sucker stay on the tomato plant, it will grow and produce branches and suckers, flowers and fruits, just like a regular tomato plant. For propagation purposes, you want to select a healthy sucker that is at least 6 to 8 inches (15 to 20 cm) tall. You can totally do this with any sized sucker, but a larger one works best for replanting later in the garden.

Use a clean and sharp pair of pruners and snip at a slight angle. Avoid using scissors as it can crush the stem.

Step 2: Propagate in a Jar of Water.

Take the snipped sucker, strip off the leaves from the bottom few inches of the stem, and immediately place it in a glass or jar of fresh water. Avoid having leaves submerged under the water as it can decompose and rot and make the water smelly. Ideally, change the water every 2 days (or more often if the water looks murky). Roots will start developing over the next 7 to 10 days and you will have a new seedling that's ready to be planted in the garden.

Place a tomato sucker in water for a few days and you can see roots starting to appear.

Once roots appear on a propagated tomato sucker, plant it in the garden and you'll have a new tomato plant for free.

Step 3. Plant in the Garden.

Once the roots on your propagated tomato suckers are at least 2 inches (5 cm) long, it's time to plant in the garden. Alternatively, you could pot up the tomato sucker into a small container filled with good quality organic potting soil or even seed starting mix and let it grow bigger, before planting it in the garden. When planting the sucker in the soil, make sure that you plant them deep as tomatoes grow roots along their stems. Amend the planting hole with some earthworm castings for gentle nutrition. Keep the plant well watered to prevent the soil from drying out (which could stress the plant). Don't forget to add a label and properly stake/support your newly propagated tomato plant.

When propagating and multiplying tomato plants, please keep in mind that your seedling will produce tomatoes a bit later during the season as it will need time to grow and mature. Hence the ideal time to propagate tomato suckers is usually in early summer. Hope you try this easy and simple trick and grow more plants and food for free!

How to Propagate and Multiply Herbs

Want to grow an endless supply of your favorite herbs for free? Herbs like basil, mint, scallions, rosemary, thyme, oregano, lavender, sage, stevia, and more can easily be multiplied via a technique called propagation, which involves taking a cutting from the parent plant, rooting it in water or soil, and growing a brand new plant. You can repeat this process over and over again and have fresh herbs all year round. Here's how to do it:

1   Using a pair of sharp scissors, cut a 4- to 6-inch-long (10 to 15 cm) stem of your favorite herb, leaving small baby leaves intact on the parent plant to continue growing and branching out. When making cuttings, ensure that the stem that you're cutting isn't diseased or flowering. Also ensure that the stem is not old, brown, and hard but fresh, soft, and pliable.

2   Next, strip off the leaves from the bottom 2 inches (5 cm) of the stem.

3   Place the cutting in a glass of water making sure that no leaves are submerged under water; otherwise, they will rot and become smelly.

4   Place this glass on a sunny windowsill.

5   Change the water every 2 days, or more often if it looks cloudy or murky.

6   Roots should start developing in just 7 to 10 days.

Once the roots are about 1 to 2 inches (2.5 to 5 cm) long, you can transplant the cutting into a well-draining pot or container that's filled with rich, fluffy, organic soil. You can also transplant directly into the garden too, if the weather is suitable.

Soft-stemmed herbs such as basil should be propagated in water, while woody-stemmed herbs such as rosemary, sage, and lavender should be propagated in soil.

Many gardeners suggest directly planting a cutting in soil instead of first rooting it in water. I've personally found it challenging as optimal conditions such as soil moisture levels and a sterile medium are needed to enable growth of roots and prevent soilborne disease from killing the tender cutting. If you do wish to try it, you can dip the cut part of the cutting in some rooting powder or rooting hormone before placing it in soil.

Step 1: Take cuttings of basil stems that are not flowering or diseased. Cut a 4- to 6-inch-long (10 to 15 cm) stem, leaving small baby leaves intact on the mother plant to continue growing.

Step 2: Strip off the leaves from the bottom 2 inches (5 cm) and submerge the stem in water. Make sure leaves are not submerged in the water.

Lastly, keep in mind that many herbs can take a long time to grow from seed, so multiplying your herbs via propagation from cuttings is a faster way to grow a new plant.

Step 3: Roots should start developing in 7 to 10 days. This basil cutting has grown really large roots in water. Transplant into a well-draining container with rich, organic soil when roots are 1 to 2 inches (2.5 to 5 cm) long.

Growing Sweet Potato Slips

Do you have some old sweet potatoes lying in your pantry that are sprouting little buds? Great news is that you can use them to grow more sweet potatoes for free! Sweet potatoes are grown by planting "slips" that are easily developed from those very same sprouting taters. Below is a step-by-step guide on how to grow your own sweet potato slips in under 10 days.

Step 1: Choose the Right Sweet Potato.

For the purpose of growing slips, you need to choose organic sweet potatoes from the grocery store that have tiny little sprouts developing on them. If you don't see little sprouts or buds, then place the sweet potatoes in a dark, dry spot in the pantry or closet for 2 to 3 weeks to facilitate this process.

Step 2: Bury It.

Once you see tiny buds growing on your sweet potato, go ahead and partially bury it in premoistened seed starting mix. The sprouted bits need to be buried no more than 1 inch (2.5 cm) deep in soil. Reuse your old plastic containers, shoeboxes, or aluminum foil trays for this purpose. No need to make drainage holes at the bottom.

Step 3: Provide Warmth and Moisture.

I've found that placing your container on top of a heat mat and covering it with a humidity dome (or cling wrap) greatly speeds up the sprouting process and produces slips quickly. You will see shoots (slips) start to form in less than a week. Since the sweet potatoes are on a heat mat, I recommend misting the soil with water as needed because you don't want to let it dry out completely. Once slips are 1 inch (2.5 cm) tall, you can take the container off the heat mat and place it under grow lights or on a sunny windowsill.

Step 4: Detach Slips and Root Them in Water.

Detach slips when they are at least 4 inches (10 cm) tall and have at least three sets of leaves on them. You can pluck them off the main or "mother" sweet potato and place them in individual jars of water on a sunny windowsill or under grow lights to propagate and develop roots.

Step 5: Plant.

Plant your rooted slips in good quality soil 2 to 3 weeks after your last frost date, or once nighttime temps are consistently over 50°F (10°C).

Enjoy your harvest after 90 to 100 days! Psst: Did you know that the leaves of sweet potato vines are edible?

Bury a sprouting organic sweet potato in soil and shoots will start to grow.

I've used an old plastic shoebox to grow sweet potato slips.

Detach individual slips when they are over 4 inches (10 cm) tall.

Place sweet potato slips in individual glasses of water to form roots before transplanting them in the garden.

Liquid fertilizers can be absorbed faster than granular fertilizers.

Chapter 4

USING FERTILIZERS & AMENDMENTS

J ust the way our human bodies require both macro- and micronutrients to thrive, plants do too. Most of these essential nutrients can be found in healthy soil and compost. However, there are plenty of fertilizers and amendments available in the market today that can help boost soil fertility and plant health and support you in your gardening journey of food abundance.

Before adding fertilizers and amendments to the garden, a great place to start is with a soil test so you know which nutrients are in abundance and those that are lacking. Ideal soil for vegetable gardening is one that has the right amount of macronutrients such as nitrogen, phosphorus, and potassium, is rich in micronutrients like calcium, magnesium, and iron, and has a pH of 6.5 and a loamy consistency (balanced amount of clay, silt, and sand).

In this chapter, you will learn about the different types of fertilizers, what NPK values mean, how and when to fertilize your plants, and how to use compost in the garden and add essential micronutrients to your soil. Did you know that you can add different fertilizers at different stages of a plant's life cycle in order to achieve specific results (such as leafy green growth or root/bulb development or to boost flower and fruit production)?

At the end of the day, as gardeners, our goal should be to maximize production while simultaneously creating a healthy ecosystem where beneficial organisms and plants can thrive.

Leafy green vegetables like kale grow well with a fertilizer that's high in nitrogen (N).

I recommend adding a fertilizer high in phosphorus (P), such as rock dust or bone meal, when planting root vegetables like garlic. It greatly helps with bulb and root development.

What Does NPK on Fertilizer Bags Mean?

N, P, and K stand for nitrogen, phosphorus, and potassium, respectively—macro nutrients that are essential for a plant's growth and health. Think about it this way—just the way our human bodies need the right amounts of macronutrients such as protein, carbohydrates, and fat for our health and well-being, plants need macronutrients in the form of nitrogen (N), phosphorus (P), and potassium (K) in the right proportions to thrive and produce.

If you pick up any bag of fertilizer from the shelf, you will most likely see three numbers listed on it such as 10-10-10 or 3-4-4 or 4-3-3, etc. The first number will always represent the percentage of nitrogen, the second number represents phosphorus, and the last or third number represents potassium in the fertilizer. A fertilizer that has all the three macronutrients of nitrogen, phosphorus, and potassium (NPK) in equal amounts (for example: 5-5-5 or 10-10-10 or 20-20-20, etc.) is considered an all-purpose fertilizer or a balanced fertilizer. Let's explore how these three macronutrients can help in your vegetable garden.

1 Nitrogen (N).

Nitrogen is an essential nutrient that helps with leafy green growth in plants. A fertilizer high in nitrogen works best when growing leafy vegetables, such as lettuce, mustards, bok choy, spinach, kale, and cabbage. It also works well during the early stages of a plant's life cycle when seedlings are small and need to put out new leafy growth, which in turn brings more energy to the plant. Examples of organic fertilizers that are high in nitrogen are composted horse, chicken, or poultry manure; feather meal; cottonseed meal; urea, bat guano, and earthworm castings. Amendments like fish emulsion and blood meal are also very high in nitrogen but are derived from animal sources.

2 Phosphorus (P).

Phosphorus is an incredible nutrient that helps not only with root growth but also helps in the development of flowers, blooms, and fruits. I usually amend my soil with a fertilizer high in phosphorus prior to planting garlic bulbs and carrots or other root vegetables. I also scratch it in at the base of my tomato, pepper, cucumber, or other fruiting plants when I see them start to set out blooms. I only do this once or twice a season, not more frequently. A few examples of high phosphorus fertilizers are rock phosphate and bone meal (the latter being derived from animal sources).

3 Potassium (K).

Potassium is an excellent nutrient for the vigor and vitality of plants and helps in the photosynthesis and transpiration process (exchange of air and water vapor from the leaves). It also helps with healthy root development. If you're growing from seed indoors, you may have noticed that the leaves on your tomato plants sometimes turn purple when you harden them off. This can happen because of a potassium deficiency —most likely because cold temperatures prevent the seedling from absorbing the potassium it needs. Compost, kelp meal, liquid kelp, greensand, wood ash, and potash are all great sources of potassium. Prior to fertilizing your plants with potassium, I recommend doing a soil test as excess potassium can result in stunted growth in plants and prevent the absorption of other essential nutrients.

I fertilize my raised beds once every 2 weeks with earthworm casting tea for gentle, organic nutrition.

Apply a fertilizer that's high in phosphorus (P) when you see flowers start to appear on the plant.

When to Fertilize Plants

First things first—there isn't any rule that says you *have to* fertilize your plants. It's simply a matter of choice and preference and depends on the condition and productivity of your vegetable garden. Most plants will produce and grow just fine if you plant them in healthy soil and don't deprive them of water. However, if you've been gardening for several years, planting crops in the same area, then over time nutrients will get depleted from the soil. This is when fertilizers come in handy.

Also keep in mind that fruiting and flowering plants, such as tomatoes, cucumbers, squash, melons, peppers, and eggplants, are usually hungry feeders and have more nutritional requirements when compared to quick maturing crops with shallow root systems, such as leafy greens, lettuce, arugula, radishes, and herbs. Plants that take longer to grow and mature, such as cauliflowers, cabbages, broccoli, and potatoes, (75 to 100 days from seed to harvest) can also benefit from the use of fertilizers.

Refrain from overfertilizing your plants, especially at the seedling stage, to avoid burning roots or causing plants to wilt and die from the shock of excess amounts of certain nutrients. As often as possible, use organic products so chemical residues and salts don't leach into the soil and create an unhealthy habitat for soil life and microbes. Finally, make sure to read and follow package instructions.

1 Time of Planting Seedlings.

- Prior to planting, I gently fluff up the top 4 to 6 inches (10 to 15 cm) of soil with a hand rake or trowel to loosen up any compacted soil. Don't dig too deep as you want to avoid disturbing beneficial soil biology and earthworms.

- After fluffing up the soil, add 3 to 4 inches (8 to 10 cm) of compost on top. Don't mix it in because the nutrients from the top will seep into the soil at root level every time you water the garden or when it rains.

- Next, dig your planting hole and add into it some earthworm castings for gentle nutrition, a handful of organic all-purpose fertilizer for overall growth. Sprinkle mycorrhizae fungi on the roots of your seedlings for soil association to help roots grow big and strong.

- Plant the seedling, water deeply, and your vegetable garden will be all set to thrive over the growing season.

2 Flowering/Mid-Season.

Another good time to fertilize your plants is when you notice flowers on your summer crops, such as tomatoes, cucumbers, eggplants, peppers, melons, and squash. "Side dress" your plants by adding a fertilizer around the base of the plant that's high in phosphorus (P), which encourages flowers to set fruit.

3 Growing in Pots/Containers.

Crops that are grown in containers need to be fertilized more often when compared to those grown in raised beds or in the ground. This is because containers hold a limited amount of soil, which limits the amount of nutrients that plants have access to. When growing in containers, make sure that you fertilize your plants weekly.

4 Signs of Stress.

Finally, if you notice signs of stress on your plants, such as yellowing leaves or stunted growth, fertilize with some compost, worm castings, or earthworm casting tea to gently nourish your plants.

How to Fertilize Plants

Fertilizers come in a variety of formulations—from granular or slow release to liquid, which are considered fast absorbing. Fertilizers can also be mild and gentle or come in a super concentrated form. Before applying them to your garden, keep in mind that stronger, concentrated formulations can possibly burn the roots of your plants, so apply with caution and read the package instructions carefully. There's nothing worse than accidentally killing your plant when the intention is to do the opposite. Here are some tips on how I apply different fertilizers in my vegetable garden.

Fertilizing plants with a liquid foliar feed helps plants absorb nutrients very quickly. Apply early in the morning or late evening to avoid leaf burn.

1 Side Dress.

It's important to fertilize your plants mid-season so that they have continuous access to nutrients to thrive and produce big harvests for you. To do this, simply push aside any straw or mulch that might be covering the top of your soil, sprinkle some granular fertilizer around the base of the plant, and gently scratch it into the top inch or two of the soil using a hand rake. Place the mulch back and water well. When applying granular fertilizers, make sure that you sprinkle them at least 1 to 2 inches (2.5 to 5 cm) away from the stem. You can do the same side-dressing routine with compost and earthworm castings too.

2 Foliar Spray.

Did you know that many organic liquid fertilizers can be added to water and used as foliar spray on the leaves of the plant? Liquid kelp, compost tea, comfrey tea, and fish emulsion are often used as foliar sprays with great effectiveness as nutrients get absorbed via the stomata of the leaves. Apply early morning or late evening when leaves are most open and receptive (versus limp/droopy in the hot afternoon sun). Foliar sprays are great because they give an immediate boost to the plant.

3 Soil Drench.

Another easy way to fertilize your plants is by using water soluble fertilizers, diluting them as per the package instructions and watering your garden soil with it. This is another quick way to make nutrients available to your plant easily. I often do this when using earth-

I don't fertilize peas, beans, and plants in the legume family as they fix nitrogen from the atmosphere and add it back into the soil.

worm casting tea, liquid kelp/seaweed or other organic liquid fertilizers. Liquid fertilizers can be used once every 2 weeks for optimum growth. However, when growing food in containers, I recommend fertilizing with liquid fertilizers once every week, especially when growing fruiting vegetables such as tomatoes, peppers, eggplants, etc.

The only time I recommend not fertilizing your plants is when growing beans, peas, legumes, or cover crops. Also avoid fertilizing root vegetables (unless it's an application of high-phosphorus fertilizer at the time of planting) as too much nitrogen can lead to leafy green growth and not sufficient root growth (see page 84 for Why Do I Have Only Leaves and No Radishes?).

Using Compost in the Garden

Compost is often known as black gold or a gardener's best friend! And with good reason. It's the one amendment that can single handedly transform your gardening game and I can't rave enough about it. Whether you choose to buy compost in bulk from your local soil yard or make your own homemade compost from kitchen scraps, it's an amendment that you must add to your vegetable garden each year. Good quality compost looks like soil, smells sweet like the earth, and is high in organic matter like composted leaves, composted animal manure, broken down food scraps, and possibly worm castings as well (if you do vermicomposting). Here's how to use compost in your garden for best results.

1   Apply in Autumn.

The best time to apply compost to your garden is in fall, after removing spent summer plants and cleaning up/removing garden debris, diseased leaves, and fallen and rotting fruits. This is because the compost will get a chance to further break down over the winter months, adding nutrients to your soil, providing a source of food for the earthworms and soil microbiology to thrive on, while also acting as mulch to insulate the soil and any fall/winter crops growing in the colder months.

Once you've cleaned up the garden or your raised beds, gently fluff up the top 4 to 6 inches (10 to 15 cm) of your existing soil which most likely would have compacted over the growing season. Next, apply 2 to 4 inches (5 to 10 cm) of compost on top of the soil. Do not mix it in; simply layer it on top. This will allow the nutrients to slowly seep into the soil over time, ensuring that your vegetable garden is prepped and ready by springtime (translating into less work for you).

2   Apply in Spring.

Another great time to apply compost to your garden is in springtime, prior to planting your spring/summer crops. This is especially important if you're like me and grow food in your garden over the colder months of fall and winter. You will want to replenish the nutrients in your soil and ensure that it's prepped and ready for heavy feeders, such as brassicas, tomatoes, cucumbers, zucchini, peppers, eggplants, potatoes, etc. Do the same drill—clean up your existing garden soil first, fluff up the top few inches to loosen up the soil that may have compacted over winter, and then add a layer of compost on top (avoid mixing it in).

My homemade compost is made from kitchen scraps and fruit and vegetable peels and is teeming with earthworms. I apply it to my raised beds each fall.

Harvesting fresh compost from my tumbling style composter.

3 Use as Mulch.

I highly recommend using compost as a mulch around your cold-hardy crops, when growing food in fall and winter. I plant garlic 2 weeks before my first frost date, and once the shoots have sprouted and are about 2 to 4 inches (5 to 10 cm) tall, I apply mushroom compost around the base of the plants. I do the same to my carrot seedlings too. The wonderful thing about mulching with compost is that it insulates the soil, delays the ground from getting frozen solid, and keeps the root veggies warm and thriving for a longer time in the colder months. The best part is that compost also provides gentle nutrition to the crops in your fall/winter garden, which helps them grow really well.

Adding Micronutrients to the Soil

When talking about fertilizers and nutrients for a vegetable garden, many people only think of N, P, and K (nitrogen, phosphorus, and potassium, respectively). Yes, those are the most important essential nutrients that plants need to grow. However, several micronutrients and trace minerals are required by the plants, albeit in smaller quantities, to boost health and productivity of the vegetable garden. Some of these micronutrients are calcium, iron, zinc, magnesium, boron, chlorine, copper, molybdenum, and sulfur, just to name a few. Below, I'm listing three key micronutrients that will make the biggest difference to your garden.

1   Rock Dust.

Rock dust is one of my favorite amendments to add to the garden each year. It is high in trace minerals, such as magnesium, manganese, iron, and more, boosts the growth and production of plants, and doesn't burn the roots. There are two types of rock dusts available in the market today: volcanic rock dust (often known as AZOMITE) and glacial rock dust. AZOMITE is mined from volcanic ash deposits and is known to contain over seventy trace minerals. The name AZOMITE is actually an acronym that stands for: A to Z Of Minerals Including Trace Elements. Glacial rock dust is created when parts of rocks erode due to glacial activity, so it is very high in minerals and micronutrients and helps to re-mineralize the soil.

You can apply rock dust by sprinkling several handfuls and mixing it in with your soil, compost, or bagged potting mixes prior to planting.

2   Calcium.

Calcium is a key element that will not only make a fruit or vegetable more nutritious but will also help with root and stem development. You usually know that your soil is lacking in calcium when you notice signs of stunted growth, wilting of leaves, and blossom end rot (black spot often found at the bottom of your tomatoes). Before adding calcium to the soil, it's best to send a sample of your soil for testing. This is because the addition of calcium can often alter the pH of the soil.

Good sources of calcium are bone meal, dolomite lime (which can increase the pH of the soil and make it more alkaline), gypsum (which can lower the pH and make it more acidic), and my favorite: composted bananas or banana peels as well as composted eggshells. Many people suggest adding whole eggs or eggshells into the planting hole. However, since they take several years to break down and become bioavailable for the plants, in my experience, it's best to pulverize eggshells and add it to your compost pile and then add that broken down compost into your garden.

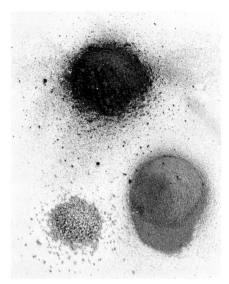

Clockwise from top: Earthworm castings, greensand, and mycorrhizal fungi are three superb micronutrients for your plants.

One of the reasons why I'm able to grow a healthy and productive organic garden each year is because of the addition of micronutrients like mycorrhizal fungi and rock dust into the garden each year.

3 Mycorrhizal Fungi.

Even though mycorrhizal fungus is technically not considered a micronutrient, it is extremely beneficial to root growth and development. Mycorrhizal fungi create a symbiotic relationship with the plants, where the fungi enable the roots to better access moisture and nutrients from the soil, and in turn, plants provide the fungi with carbohydrates and sugars created during the photosynthesis process.

Mycorrhizal fungus is often sold in granular or powder form and is sprinkled on to the roots of plants at the time of planting. Fungal-dominated compost (example: composted leaves or leaf mold, broken down wood chips, and compost made through the cold composting process) can also be applied to the soil to add mycelium/mycorrhizae fungi to it.

Yes, pests and diseases can be found in every vegetable garden, but catching the problem early and managing it is the key to success.

Chapter 5

MANAGING PESTS & DISEASES

Growing your own food is one of the greatest joys of life, but it's no fun when you have to constantly deal with pests and diseases that make you almost want to give up on gardening. Worry not, in this chapter, I'll be discussing the most common pests and diseases that you can find in your vegetable garden and easy, organic remedies to manage and control them effectively.

I want you to remember that creating a garden also means building an ecosystem where both good bugs and bad bugs live. You cannot have one without the other and that's part of the way nature works. Also know that homegrown food that's pristine and perfect is a myth and unfortunately the idea of perfectionism is further reinforced into our society by the perfect produce that you see at the grocery store.

I usually follow a three-pronged approach when it comes to fighting pests and diseases: First, regularly check your plants for signs of stress and disease. It's easier to solve a problem that has just begun versus trying to fight a battle when pests or diseases have taken complete control over your plant.

Second, always target your problem with the most gentle approach first. A simple jet spray of water helps dislodge most pests, or simply pick them off the plant if possible.

Third, prune or trim off diseased or infected leaves to prevent the spread from one plant to another. When growing a vegetable garden, also remember to grow flowers and pollinator-friendly plants, to attract natural predators and other beneficial insects that will prey on the unwanted pests. For simple organic remedies on pest management in your garden, read on.

Calendula is a fantastic trap crop for attracting aphids.

Last year I was very surprised to see that cabbage loopers feasted on my red cabbage plant (trap crop) but left the kale plants alone.

How to Use Trap Crops

For centuries organic farmers have used the strategy of planting "trap crops," also known as sacrificial crops, to keep pesky bugs away from their cash crops. These are crops that you plant to attract pests and insects, so they feast on them and leave your main plant alone. Think of them as companion plants, sacrificial plants, decoy plants, or beneficial plants for your garden.

The biggest advantage of using trap crops is that it reduces the need to use chemicals and pesticides in the vegetable garden.

My Favorite Trap Crops

Trap Crop	Pests It Attracts
Calendula	Aphids
Marigold	Aphids, Root Nematodes
Nasturtium	Aphids
Collards	Cabbage Moths
Blue Hubbard Squash	Cucumber Beetles, Squash Vine Borers
Four O'Clock Flowers	Japanese Beetles

Follow the guidelines below when using trap crops as a pest control strategy.

1   Trap Crops Need to be Well Established.

Keep in mind that the crop that you wish to sacrifice should be larger and more mature than the plant that it's trying to protect. For example, a small calendula plant with barely any flowers on it will not be able to effectively protect your tomato plant from being attacked by aphids.

2   Plant Trap Crops Around the Borders.

I highly recommend planting sacrificial crops on the edges and borders of your raised beds or vegetable patch. It creates a first line of defense, sort of like pawns on a chessboard to protect the more valuable crops inside, such as tomatoes, cucumbers, etc. I love planting marigolds, calendula, and nasturtiums along the borders/edges of my raised beds to create this barrier.

3   Remove Trap Crop that Is Infested with Pests.

Once you notice that the trap crop is infested with pests, make sure that you remove or discard it quickly. You could also choose to use organic pest control products on the trap crop to smother and kill the pests in question. Keep in mind that if you wait too long to remove the affected trap crop, pests will move from a spent trap crop onto a healthy main crop and start feasting on it.

What Are the Best Companion Plants?

Onion seedlings planted between rows of lettuce help deter aphids with their strong smell.

Companion planting is the concept of growing mutually beneficial crops next to one another, not just for pest resistance but also to boost growth and flavor of the plants.

To adopt companion planting in your garden, embrace the concept of polyculture, where you plant a variety of herbs, flowers, and vegetables together, which not only confuses and deters pests but also attracts pollinators and adds color and beauty too. Below are my top three favorite companion plants to include in a vegetable garden.

1 Garlic.

The strong, pungent smell and flavor of garlic is unmistakable and repels a lot of pests, including aphids, Japanese beetles, spider mites, and cabbage loopers too. In fact, you might find garlic used as an ingredient in many organic pest control products sold on the market. Garlic is compatible with most plants, except peas, beans, and legumes.

2 Rosemary.

Another fantastic companion herb is rosemary, which should be planted next to brassicas like kale, cabbage, cauliflower, Brussels sprouts, broccoli, radishes, etc. The strong smell of rosemary confuses the cabbage moth butterfly and therefore can save your brassicas from being decimated by caterpillars. Avoid planting rosemary next to cucumber, squash, and melon plants as excessive watering (which cucurbits like) can hurt your rosemary plant; it likes drier conditions.

3 Calendula.

Calendula belongs to the aster family and is an excellent medicinal flower and companion plant to almost all crops. The flower excretes a sticky residue called resin that is very effective in trapping aphids and whiteflies. Plant calendula next to tomatoes, potatoes, cucumbers, beans, and pretty much any crop in your vegetable garden.

Companion Planting Cheat Sheet

Plant	Friend	Foe
Tomato	Basil, borage, marigold, calendula, garlic, onion, chives, beans, beets, Swiss chard, lettuce, peppers, sage, thyme, parsley	Potato, corn, brassicas, dill
Cucumber	Dill, borage, onion, oregano, marigold, nasturtiums, chives, beans, peppers, radish	Sage, potatoes
Pepper	Cucumber, tomato, basil, marigold, onion, parsley, oregano, marjoram, Swiss chard	Beans, brassicas
Eggplant	Marigold, nasturtiums, tomatoes, peppers	None
Carrot	Onion, garlic, chives, lettuce, beans, peas, tomatoes, sage	Dill, cilantro
Brassicas	Garlic, onion, dill, nasturtiums, marigold, sage, oregano, beets	Pole beans
Corn	Pole beans, squash, cucumber, melons, potatoes, spinach, sunflower, sage, thyme	Tomato, brassicas
Beans	Rosemary, thyme, sage, nasturtiums, strawberries, tomatoes, corn, Swiss chard, beets	Garlic, onion, chives,
Peas	Strawberry, mint, parsley, radish, spinach, sage, thyme, cucumber, carrots, beans	Garlic, onion, chives
Allium	Allium (garlic, onion, chives, leeks, scallions)	Beans, peas, legumes, sage
Lettuce	Onion, garlic, chives, scallion, leeks, spinach, peas, brassicas	None
Spinach	Cilantro, sage, thyme, oregano, rosemary, peas, beans, brassicas, lettuce, strawberries	None
Potato	Marigold, beans, calendula, cilantro	Beans
Squash	Corn, beans, peas, marigold, nasturtium	Potatoes, brassicas

Aphids hiding on the underside of tomato leaves.

Using tape to catch aphids.

Getting Rid of Aphids

Aphids are the bane of every gardener's existence. They are one of the most common pests that you'll find in a veggie garden. Aphids are small, soft-bodied insects that suck the juices from your plants, stunting their growth, turning leaves yellow, and even, in extreme cases, killing your plant. Aphids come in a variety of colors (I've personally seen green, white, and reddish-brown ones in my own garden), and they typically hide on the undersides of the leaves or within the curls or folds of a plant. Upon sucking the sap of the plant, aphids secrete a sticky substance called honeydew, which is a very desirable snack to ants. If you see a lot of ants in your garden, hovering around your plants, it's usually an indication of an aphid infestation. You can always go leaf by leaf and remove or squish the aphids by hand, but here are some easier, less time-consuming ways to get rid of them.

1 Jet of Water.

Because aphids are soft-bodied insects, using a jet spray of water from your hose will not only dislodge them from the plant, but will also render them incapacitated. This method is most useful in the beginning, when you see only a few aphids in your garden. This is also the ideal strategy for young plants or seedlings that are still tender and for whom spraying with organic pest control products may be too harsh.

2 Neem Oil and Pure Castile Soap Spray.

If you're facing a larger aphid infestation, it might be a good idea to spray your plants, particularly the undersides of leaves, with a combination of neem oil and pure Castile liquid soap. See page 134 for more information about neem oil, including the recipe I use to spray my plants.

3 Tape.

If you wish to avoid spraying your plants with neem oil or pest control products, then take some tape (a lint roller works too) and use it to get rid of the aphids by trapping them on the sticky surface. This method can be time-consuming and is doable for those with smaller gardens.

4 Beneficial Insects.

Welcome beneficial insects such as ladybugs, lacewings, and hoverflies into your garden. They love feasting on aphids, which means you need to do less work to control these pests. Plants like flowering dill, cilantro, parsley, marigolds, and calendula attract these beneficial insects, so plant plenty of them in your vegetable garden.

Did you know that one ladybug can eat up to 50 to 75 aphids in a day? Welcome them in your garden by planting herbs and flowers.

Preventing Blight on Tomato Plants

Blight on tomato plants can easily be recognized by leaves that develop brown spots on them and fruits that rot before they are ready for harvest. These fungal spores are exacerbated by humid conditions and spread very easily from one plant to another via the wind. It is essential to curtail it as soon as you notice the first signs of this disease.

Late blight on my tomato plants usually occurs near the end of summer. When the spread is rampant, I harvest any remaining tomatoes, including green ones, and then discard the plant.

Types of Blight and Remedies

Early Blight	Early blight can occur anytime during the plant's life cycle and can be identified by concentric brown rings on the leaves. It is very important to get rid of the affected leaves as soon as possible because if diseased foliage falls to the ground, blight spores can survive in the soil and overwinter only to return and infect tomato (and potato) plants the next year.
Late Blight	Luckily, the spores of late blight cannot survive in the soil; however, they can spread rapidly through the wind. This disease is characterized by rotting and moldy-looking fruit and browning, curling leaves that look like they are drying up and dying.
Septoria Leaf Spot	This is another kind of blight that is identified by multiple small brown spots on your tomato leaves, which can overwinter in the soil, just like early blight.

Here are the best tried-and-true strategies to prevent blight on your tomato plants.

1 Variety Selection.

When buying tomato seeds, look for varieties that are blight resistant. It won't make them completely immune but will certainly offer some degree of resistance. Look for codes that say: EB (Early Blight), LB (Late Blight), and AB (Alternaria Blight).

2 Pruning.

Good air circulation is super important when it comes to keeping tomato plants healthy and preventing blight. Lack of airflow leads to an environment of high humidity, which encourages fungal growth, i.e., blight.

3 Mulching.

Adding 1 to 2 inches (2.5 to 5 cm) of mulch on top of the soil helps prevent soil from splashing back on to the plants and prevents the spread of early blight and septoria leaf spot. A great mulch to use is clean straw. I like triple shredded straw as well.

4 Fungicide.

Organic fungicides can often be used to combat blight. However, I've found these are more effective as a preventive measure rather than as a cure.

HOMEMADE FUNGICIDE RECIPE
Using baking soda or potassium bicarbonate

Ingredients:

1 gallon (3.8 L) of water

1 tablespoon (15 g) baking soda or potassium bicarbonate

2 tablespoons (30 ml) pure Castile soap or 1 tablespoon (15 ml) dish soap

2 tablespoons (30 ml) vegetable oil

Application:

Mix the ingredients in a spray bottle or pump sprayer.

Apply on top and bottom of leaves.

Use early morning or late evening.

Apply once a week.

Avoiding Blossom End Rot

Have you ever grown a tomato that looks perfect on top, but has a rotting black spot at the bottom? This is a tell-tale sign of blossom end rot. Blossom end rot most commonly affects tomatoes but can also happen to peppers, eggplants, cucumber, squash, and melons too.

The main reason why blossom end rot occurs in fruiting plants is due to calcium deficiency. A lot of people think that this happens because their soil itself is lacking in calcium, but more often than not it's inconsistent watering (too little or too much), which prevents the plants from properly absorbing calcium and other nutrients from the soil.

Unfortunately, once a fruit develops blossom end rot, it cannot be reversed. However, certain simple measures can be taken proactively to prevent it from happening in the first place and to ensure that subsequent fruits grown on that plant don't develop blossom end rot.

Here are some tips to avoid blossom end rot and get a good harvest.

1   Consistent Watering.

The most common reason for the occurrence of blossom end rot is inconsistent watering. Both underwatering and overwatering stresses the plant and it is unable to absorb calcium that is available to it in the soil. Don't allow the soil to dry out too much between watering, and at the same time, don't saturate the soil with excessive water. The key is to have a regular watering schedule. Installing a drip irrigation system can help with this, ensuring that the plant gets a sufficient amount of water at regular intervals.

2   Mulching.

Adding mulch on top of the soil prevents the evaporation of water and helps it retain moisture, which is especially important in the heat of summer. Make sure to add 1 to 2 inches (2.5 to 5 cm) of mulch on top of your soil. Don't mix it in. For more information on mulching, read Using Mulch on page 70.

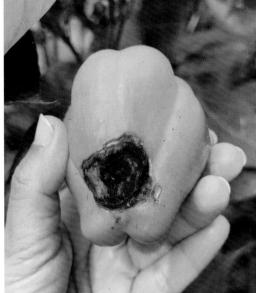

Blossom end rot on tomatoes is usually a sign that the plant is unable to absorb calcium due to irregular watering or a deficiency in the soil.

Blossom end rot can occur in peppers too, not just in tomatoes.

3   Calcium Supplement.

Sometimes blossom end rot can indeed occur due to a calcium deficiency in the soil. The best way to find out is by sending a soil sample for testing at your local cooperative extension. If the soil is lacking in calcium, then you can supplement it by adding organic garden lime or gypsum to your soil. You can also use bone meal too, but it is an animal byproduct and is considered a slow-release fertilizer. When it comes to lime, please keep in mind that it can alter the pH of your soil and make it more alkaline, so exercise caution before using it. Gypsum is made of 20 percent calcium and 16 percent sulfur but is pH neutral. Both lime and gypsum are water soluble and can be quickly absorbed by the plants.

A good way to add calcium to the soil is by adding crushed or pulverized eggshells into the compost or in your garden every year in autumn. Eggshells are very high in calcium. However, since they take a long time to break down, it's best to add them to your garden each fall. Doing this regularly each year will ensure that you're building soil health over time.

Spider mites are hard to find because they are so small. Look for tell-tale signs such as webbing and stippling of leaves.

Getting Rid of Spider Mites

Apart from aphids, spider mites are perhaps one of the most common and dreaded pests in the garden. Why? Because unlike other insects, they are almost impossible to see with the naked eye. They are as small as a grain of sand and some people even use a magnifying glass to find them! They damage the plant by sucking the sap and life juices out and leaves start turning yellow and dull. Spider mites are notorious for multiplying rapidly and moving together in colonies, almost like an army.

If you notice dull, yellowing leaves that seem to take on a bronzed appearance or stippled and mottled leaves that look like dust has settled on them and fine webbing in between, then spider mites may be to blame. They come in different colors: red, brown, or green and are most prolific during the heat of summer, especially during a dry spell.

Before you decide that your plant can't be saved, give these organic remedies a try to manage and control a spider mite infestation.

1   Rubbing Alcohol.

The most effective remedy to ge rid of spider mites is to mix 1 part rubbing alcohol with 3 parts water, dab on a cotton ball, and wipe it over the affected leaves and stem. This will kill the mites on contact. Leave on for an hour and then rinse the residue and dead mites by washing them off with water from a hose. As always, please do a test application on a small section of the plant and use in the early morning or late evening to prevent leaf burn.

2   Soap Spray.

Another great option is to spray a soapy water solution on the affected leaves. Add 4 to 5 tablespoons (60 to 75 ml) of Dr. Bronner's Peppermint Castile Soap in a gallon (3.8 L) of water. Shake thoroughly and spray on top and underside of leaves

When spider mites attack a plant, the leaves start to look stippled. Many people think it's dust, when in fact it's spider mite damage.

and stems too if they are affected. Repeat every 3 days and apply spray early in the morning or late in the evening. If you choose to use liquid dish soap instead, then use less soap (1 to 2 tablespoons per gallon, or 15 to 30 ml per 3.8 L of water) as it can be quite strong/harsh when compared to Castile soap. Finally, you could also purchase organic insecticidal soap sprays, which can help control a spider mite infestation.

3   Rosemary Oil.

Rosemary oil is an excellent organic remedy for combating spider mites in the garden. Add 2 teaspoons of pure rosemary oil to 1 gallon (3.8 L) of water and add 4 to 5 table-spoons (60 to 75 ml) of Dr. Bronner's Pure Castile Soap. Shake well and spray on the affected plants when the sun isn't too bright. Repeat every 3 days or after a rain.

Flea beetles causing damage to an eggplant plant.

Use organic pest control products responsibly. Apply late in the evening or early in the morning so beneficial insects aren't harmed in the process.

Eliminating Flea Beetles

If you see tiny black insects that look like little dots or specks all over your eggplant, tomato, or radish plants and the leaves have numerous small holes in them, then it's most likely that the pesky flea beetle is the culprit.

Flea beetles are small, black chewing insects that love to feed on plants from the nightshade family (tomato, potato, eggplant, and pepper) and brassica family too (radish, kale, bok choy, cabbage). They are hard to catch because even though they cannot fly, they hop very quickly from one plant to another.

Here are some organic remedies to control flea beetles in your vegetable garden.

1   Insect Netting/Row Covers.

Sometimes, prevention is the best medicine. If you've experienced flea beetle problems in the past, then it's very likely that they can come back to plague your plants each year as they can overwinter in soil and garden debris. The best strategy is to cover susceptible varieties with insect netting or row covers at the time of planting the seedlings. This blocks flea beetles from landing on the plant. Young seedlings are especially vulnerable to damage as they don't have too many leaves on them, and once the damage is done, it's hard for them to photosynthesize properly, causing them to wilt and die.

2 Food-Grade Diatomaceous Earth.

Diatomaceous earth (also known as DE) is a white, powdery-looking substance that looks similar to talcum powder but is a bit gritty. It's made of finely crushed fossilized algae. While DE looks like powder to our naked eye, to small pests like flea beetles, it has many sharp, jagged edges, which can scratch and cut their bodies. The dry powder also dehydrates them, causing them to die. To use, dust or sprinkle food-grade DE on leaves of the affected plant using a shaker bottle or a powder duster with an extension nozzle. Reapply after a rain as moisture will render it inactive.

A few important points to consider before using DE in your garden: Although diatomaceous earth is safe for humans and animals, inhaling the powder can be harmful to your lungs, so be sure to wear a face mask to cover your nose when using it.

Also, please use DE responsibly as it can be harmful not only to flea beetles, aphids, mites, and other soft-bodied insects, but also to beneficials like ladybugs, lacewings, and bees too (if it is sprinkled directly on them). My recommendation is to apply it late in the evening, when most bees aren't active and then cover the plant with insect netting or ag fabric to prevent bees from landing on it. DE doesn't harm earthworms and caterpillars.

3 Neem Oil Spray.

A great homemade recipe to combat flea beetles is to mix 2 teaspoons cold-pressed neem oil and 4 to 5 tablespoons (60 to 75 ml) pure Castile soap with 1 gallon (3.8 L) of water in a pump sprayer or spray bottle. Shake really well to create an emulsion and spray on top of the affected plant. Don't forget to spray the undersides of leaves too!

Since oil and water don't mix, the addition of soap is an important element in making the solution stick on the leaves and not drip off. Repeat every 3 to 5 days or after a rainfall. Spray this solution in the morning or evening as bright afternoon sunlight could burn leaves that are coated with oil and soap.

Neem oil is a great organic remedy as it not only has a powerful smell, but also tastes quite bitter, which discourages bugs from chewing on the leaves. See page 134 for more information about neem oil.

Say Goodbye to Cucumber Beetles

Cucumber beetles are bright yellow-winged beetles with either black stripes or black spots on them and are notorious for completely decimating cucurbit family crops (cucumber, squash, zucchini, and melon plants) in a matter of days, sometimes even overnight. Unfortunately, they even spread bacterial wilt in these plants and leaves end up looking droopy and wilted as though they haven't been watered and the plant ultimately dies.

I have personally lost way too many cucumber and squash seedlings to pesky cucumber beetles over the years and am sharing what I do to manage them.

1 Covering Seedlings.

The best chance that you have of saving your cucurbit family plants from being attacked by cucumber beetles is to cover your seedlings right away, at the time of planting. Use floating row covers, insect netting, or agricultural fabric to cover seedlings. Only remove the covers when you find both male and female flowers being produced on the plant, to allow for pollination to occur.

2 Companion Planting.

Cucumber beetles are attracted to the distinctive smell that's emitted from the cucurbit family plant and to their bright yellow flowers as well. So create a decoy by companion planting with herbs like dill and borage that distract the beetles with their scent and grow flowers like calendula, marigold, and nasturtiums to attract them with their brightly colored flowers.

3 Growing Self-Pollinating Varieties.

If cucumber beetles are ravaging your plants each year, try crop rotation, i.e., growing them in a different location. If that doesn't help either, then, try growing a self-pollinating cucumber variety called 'Beit Alpha', which doesn't need bees or insects to help it pollinate and grow fruit. Several gardeners grow 'Beit Alpha' in an indoor greenhouse or under row covers and do not need to remove those covers at all, except at the time of harvesting the fruit.

4 Food-Grade Diatomaceous Earth.

When growing food organically, sprinkle a dusting of food-grade diatomaceous earth (DE) on the leaves (not on the flowers) of cucurbit family plants to help control and kill cucumber beetles. Diatomaceous earth is finely crushed fossilized algae and looks like chalk powder. Not visible to the naked eye, the sharp edges of DE act like shards of glass and cut the beetle's exoskeleton, causing it to dehydrate and eventually die. Avoid using DE on flowers as bees and other beneficial insects can also be harmed. Apply late in the evening. Use a mask to avoid inhaling DE as it's harmful to our lungs too. Reapply after rain.

Yellow and black-striped cucumber beetles can decimate cucurbit family plants overnight. Using row covers on seedlings is a must, until flowers begin to appear. At that point remove the cover.

5 Delayed Planting.

Cucumber beetles are most active in late spring and early summer (usually May and June), so plant cucumbers, zucchini, and melons 2 to 4 weeks after your last frost date to make them less susceptible to damage.

Grow self-pollinating varieties of cucumber under cover to avoid cucumber beetle damage. 'Beit Alpha' is a popular variety to grow for this purpose.

6 Kaolin Clay.

Another organic way to deter cucumber beetles is by spraying young cucurbit seedlings with Surround WP kaolin clay. The clay creates a protective white coating on the plant, making it unattractive to the beetles. This strategy is most effective on freshly transplanted seedlings. Once the plants are larger and have several sets of leaves, they are more unlikely to succumb to damage. Create a kaolin clay slurry by following package directions. Application may need to be repeated after a heavy rain.

Managing Leaf Miners

Leaf miners are insects, typically larvae, that literally get inside the leaves and feed on plant tissue, leaving behind a visible trail, tunnel, or pattern. Most commonly affected plants are spinach and Swiss chard, but you can find leaf miner damage even on leaves of beans, tomato, cucumber, squash, and nasturtiums too.

As with everything else, start with preventative techniques and only use strong organic remedies when the milder ones have failed to produce results. Here's how I fight leaf miners in my garden.

1   Scrape Off Eggs/Use Sticky Tape.

Leaf miners are notorious for laying a cluster of tiny white eggs on the underside or even in the folds or curls of leaves, making them hard to find. To counteract this, make sure that every time you visit the garden, you regularly check the leaves for lurking pests and eggs. If you find leaf miner eggs, make sure to immediately scrape them off. You can also use sticky tape to get the eggs off the leaves.

2   Use Flashlight to Find Larvae.

Finding leaf miner larvae hiding inside leaf tissue can be challenging, but it's important to do in order to stop them from decimating your plants. Next time, try shining some light on the underside of the affected leaves to make them easily visible. The light makes the leaves look translucent, and it becomes really easy to spot the hidden larvae. I've use this trick all the time on my Swiss chard plants, which are most prone to damage by leaf miners. Finding leaf miner larvae is half the battle won. Squish them or prune and discard the affected leaves.

3   Row Covers.

Cover your seedlings with row covers, ag fabric, or even a light muslin cloth to prevent the leaf miner insects from laying their eggs on the plants in your garden. Every insect/pest in the garden has a life cycle, i.e., times when they are most active and times when they are least active. Leaf miners are most active during spring and early summer months from April to June. Therefore, using covers during this time will be most effective.

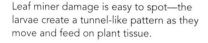

Leaf miner damage is easy to spot—the larvae create a tunnel-like pattern as they move and feed on plant tissue.

Can you spot the larvae hidden inside the Swiss chard leaf? Hold the leaf up toward the sun or use a flashlight to shine a light on the leaf and the larvae will be immediately visible.

4   Neem Oil Spray.

Insecticidal spray or neem oil spray helps combat a lot of pests in the garden, including leaf miners. Mix 2 teaspoons of cold-pressed neem oil and 4 to 5 tablespoons (60 to 75 ml) pure Castile soap with 1 gallon (3.8 L) of water in a pump sprayer or spray bottle. Shake really well to create an emulsion and spray on top of the affected leaves and on the eggs too. Repeat application once every 3 to 5 days until the infestation subsides.

Please test this spray on a small area of the plant to check for any adverse reaction before using it on the entire plant. Use this spray early in the morning or late evening, so the harsh sunlight doesn't burn the coated leaves. See page 134 for more information about neem oil.

My kale was a star attraction in the garden this year thanks to covering my baby seedlings and using organic Bt (*Bacillus thuringiensis*).

Cabbage loopers look like green caterpillars and are hard to find because they camouflage very well. When I see holes like this in my cabbage plant, I know that it is being eaten by cabbage loopers.

Preventing Holes in Kale and Brassicas

If you've ever grown kale, cabbage, broccoli, or other brassica family plants, you've probably experienced seeing leaves riddled with many holes, most likely being chewed away by small green caterpillars also known as the cabbage loopers. You may have also seen little dark green/black blobs of poop on the leaves (another giveaway sign that cabbage loopers are at work). The cabbage looper comes from the white cabbage moth butterfly and is attracted to plants in the brassica family (kale, cabbage, broccoli, cauliflower, collards, radishes, bok choy, just to name a few). It lays tiny white or light green, almost inconspicuous, eggs that look like little specks of dust on the leaves of these plants. These grow to become green caterpillars that camouflage so well that it's hard to find them until you see the damage being done to your plant. Nevertheless, there are several easy ways to prevent holes in your plants.

1 Cover Seedlings.

The number one best way to avoid cabbage loopers is by covering your brassica seedlings with floating row covers, ag fabric, muslin cloth, or insect netting at the time of planting. This physical barrier prevents the butterfly from laying its eggs on the leaves and does a wonderful job of protecting your seedlings. This is especially beneficial in spring, early summer, and early fall when cabbage moth butterflies are most active.

2 Hand Pick.

Another option is to hand pick the caterpillars off your plants and toss them somewhere far away (or feed them to your chickens). While this might seem like an effective strategy, unfortunately, it will only work if you've done a thorough job of removing every cabbage looper off your plant. Because these green caterpillars camouflage so well, sometimes it is hard to find every one of them. Nevertheless, it's worth a try.

3 Organic Bt Spray.

If you have a serious infestation, then you can spray organic Bt, also known as *Bacillus thuringiensis,* on the plant. Bt, is a naturally occurring soil bacteria that when consumed by the caterpillars causes them to die. If you buy Bt in liquid form, add the recommended amount following package directions. I highly recommend investing in a pump sprayer bottle as it will make it very easy to thoroughly apply, including on the underside of the leaves.

Please keep in mind that Bt is harmful not only to cabbage loopers but also to all caterpillars, so please use responsibly and only if necessary. Ideally use the spray late in the evening or early in the morning and apply once every 5 days.

How to Control Slugs in Your Garden

Slugs are soft-bodied mollusks that feed not only on little seedlings but also on leaves, stems, and root vegetables/tubers too! They especially love salad greens and brassicas. They have a slimy body and thrive in warm, moist/humid, and dark conditions. They can also hide very effectively in soil and mulch.

When trying to control slugs in the garden, it's best to use a combination of different remedies for maximum effectiveness.

1 Beer Trap.

Who would have thought that slugs love beer? Apparently they do! To create a beer trap, pour some beer into a shallow dish or container so it's easy for slugs to climb into and place it near the plants in your garden, in the evening. Slugs that try to drink the beer will fall and drown in it. Check the trap regularly, disposing of any captured slugs and replacing the beer as needed.

2 Copper Collars.

Another way to deter slugs from eating your plants is by placing a copper collar or copper ring around the base of your plants, forming a makeshift circular fort. It creates a physical barrier that slugs don't want to cross, because when a slug comes in contact with the copper, it receives a small electric shock that discourages it from getting near the plant. Make sure that you bury the copper ring deep under the soil too, especially at the time of planting, if slugs have been a problem in your garden. This method is considered environmentally safe as it doesn't harm other wildlife or beneficial insects.

3 Beneficial Predator Habitat.

If you have the space for it, try to create a little pond or natural habitat to attract frogs and toads into your vegetable garden. They devour slugs and will help you naturally control them.

4 Citrus Rind Trap.

If you have any leftover orange or grapefruit peels, turn them upside down and place them in the soil around your garden. Slugs love citrus, and when you flip the peel over the next day, you will find lots of snails gathered inside. Pick up and toss far away from your garden.

Slugs are so problematic in the garden. They are especially damaging to seedlings and salad greens.

Beer traps are one easy way to lure and capture slugs.

5   Avoid Watering in the Evening.

Slugs love damp, dark, and humid environments. If you water your garden in the evenings, then chances are that the soil is still moist once it gets dark and you will invariably be creating the perfect ambience for them to come and play. To manage slugs, it's best to water in the mornings/daytime so soil has a chance to dry out a bit and isn't as wet at night.

6   Plant Larger Transplants.

Slugs love munching on little seedlings. Give your plants a fighting chance to survive a slug attack by planting larger seedlings and have more ready at hand to succession plant in case they don't survive.

Making Neem Oil and Insecticidal Soap Spray

Neem oil is one of the most frequently used organic pesticides in vegetable gardening. It has a very potent, bitter flavor and pungent smell, which repels and kills many chewing insects such as aphids, spider mites, mealybugs, white flies, flea beetles, Japanese beetles, and many more. In my experience it seems to be more effective on larvae and pests that are at a younger stage in their life cycle versus adults. It is also effective as a fungicide and used in combating powdery mildew, rust, and blight to a certain extent.

What Is Neem Oil?

Neem oil is basically a type of vegetable oil that is extracted by pressing the kernels or seeds of the neem fruit, similar to how olive oil is extracted from the olive fruit. When buying neem oil, look for pure, cold-pressed oil, which tends to contain the highest amount of azadirachtin. When the compound azadirachtin is ingested by the pest, it causes changes in their hormonal cycle, which inhibits reproduction and sometimes even causes death. Neem oil spray works by coating an insect's body and smothering or suffocating it.

Is It Safe to Use?

Humans have used neem in soaps, toothpastes, and hair oils for centuries. Juice of neem leaves is considered a very powerful detoxifying agent too. While neem oil is considered organic and safe for humans, pets, and birds, it can end up being detrimental to some beneficial insects like bees, butterflies, and ladybugs only if it is sprayed directly on top of them. At the end of the day, all pesticides, organic or not, should be used responsibly and only when absolutely necessary.

Neem oil and insecticidal soap spray can not only help get rid of aphids but white fly infestation too.

What Is Insecticidal Soap?

Did you know that soapy water is incredibly effective in controlling pests and insects in the garden? Many people consider liquid dish soap (mixed with water) as an insecticidal soap. However, pure Castile soap is best as it's free of synthetic substances and additives like artificial fragrances, moisturizers, and chemicals. Insecticidal soap sprays work very well to control and kill soft-bodied insects, such as aphids, spider mites, white flies, mealybugs, thrips, and many more. Use it in combination with neem oil to make a very effective spray.

HOW TO MAKE NEEM OIL AND INSECTICIDAL SOAP SPRAY

Ingredients:

2 teaspoons cold-pressed neem oil

4–5 tablespoons (60–75 ml) pure Castile soap or peppermint-scented Castile soap

1 gallon (3.8 L) water

Pump sprayer or spray bottle

Application:

Mix neem oil and Castile soap with 1 gallon (3.8 L) of water. Shake thoroughly to emulsify and create a foamy or frothy solution. Spray on the affected plant, especially the top and underside of leaves, using a pump sprayer or a spray bottle. Repeat application 2 to 3 times per week or after a rain.

Things to Remember:

- Always do a test spray and wait 24 hours for any adverse reaction (such as leaf burn) before applying on the entire plant.

- Neem oil quickly breaks down with exposure to sunlight. Its efficacy lasts 1 to 2 days, so repeat application as needed. Do not apply in the afternoon.

- For maximum effectiveness, spray directly on top of soft-bodied insects, such as aphids, so there is actual contact with the pest. The combination of oil, soap, and water will smother and suffocate the pest.

- Apply in very early morning or preferably late evening and avoid spraying on bees.

Nothing feels better than the joy
of growing your own food!

Chapter 6

HARVEST & PRESERVE PRODUCE

After months of planning and tending to your garden, fruits, herbs, and vegetables are finally ready to be harvested and enjoyed. Most taste the best when picked at their fully ripe stage. However, some crops, such as tomatoes, can continue to ripen after harvest.

In this chapter, I will teach you different ways to harvest homegrown crops. I will also share easy storage tips so your produce can last for months, and I'll share some of my favorite recipes to make delicious sauces, pickles, and seasonings without spending hours in the kitchen. But first, here's a chart on the best time to harvest your crops.

What to Harvest	When to Harvest
Salad Greens	Pick early in the morning. Harvest individual leaves as baby greens for a sweet, tender taste.
Root Crops	When you see shoulders (top of the root veggie) peeking out from the soil, it's time to harvest. Leafy green foliage is edible too.
Tubers	Harvest when leaves start turning yellow, brown, and dying back. Baby potatoes can be harvested when the plant begins to set flowers.
Fruits	Tomatoes, melons, pumpkins, and butternut squash will taste best when picked ripe. Cucumbers, zucchini, and eggplants can be picked young for smaller seeds.
Herbs	Pick often to encourage plants to grow large and bushy.

Place blushing tomatoes next to bananas to speed up the ripening process.

Ripening Tomatoes Off the Vine

The best way to ripen tomatoes is on the vine of course—this way they have the most robust flavor and have absorbed the maximum amount of nutrients. However, as summer begins to fade and the weather starts cooling down, you will notice that tomatoes are taking a longer time to ripen on the plant. Make sure that you harvest every tomato, including the green ones, before the first frost comes. This is because tomatoes (like many other fruits) can continue to ripen even after they've been harvested. Here's how to ripen tomatoes off the vine.

1 Sorting.

Once you harvest your tomatoes, you should organize them from most ripe to least ripe. The tomatoes that are very dark green and hard will take the longest to mature and often just end up rotting or shriveling up. These should be used to make green salsa verde or fried green tomatoes. The rest of the tomatoes can be stored in a brown paper bag or cardboard box, or wrapped in newspaper or paper towels.

Avoid storing tomatoes inside zippered plastic bags as they are not breathable and will make tomatoes release their juices and rot. Finally, don't forget to inspect the fruits for blemishes. Store those separately as they can invite fungal and bacterial growth and spoil the rest of the good tomatoes too.

2 Add Apples or Bananas.

To speed up the ripening process, place one or two apples or bananas next to your unripe tomatoes inside a closed paper bag or cardboard box. These fruits release a gas called ethylene, which accelerates the ripening process. Apples release the most amount of ethylene, followed by bananas, which is why these fruits too can ripen after being picked (notice green bananas turning yellow on your kitchen counter?). Place these fruits away from direct sunlight and preferably in a dark spot.

Tomatoes that are very hard and green won't ripen off the vine and usually end up rotting. Instead, choose tomatoes that are blushing, i.e., have a slight hint of color to them.

3 Avoid Refrigeration.

By all means, do not store your unripe tomatoes in the refrigerator; otherwise, they will remain green and raw and not turn red and ripe. The only time you can refrigerate them is after they have fully ripened, to prolong their shelf life. Also avoid storing unripe tomatoes in a root cellar or basement as cool temperatures below 60°F or 16°C will slow down the ripening process. Ideally tomatoes should be stored at temperatures between 65°F to 75°F (18°C to 24°C).

Check your tomatoes every week to make sure there are no black spots or rot developing on them. Tomatoes that ripen off the vine taste just as good and can be used in fresh eating, cooking, and making salsas and sauces or whatever you wish.

An assortment of leafy greens growing in the garden: lettuce, red mustard, spinach, kale, bok choy, and more.

Rinse lettuce in a large bowl of cold water, flipping/turning the leaves multiple times. Be careful not to crush or bruise the leaves or else they won't store as well.

Harvesting Lettuce and Leafy Greens

Most fruits and vegetables taste the best when they are harvested at their mature, large, and fully ripe stage. However, lots of leafy green vegetables, such as lettuce, kale, spinach, mizuna, arugula, endive, frisée, radicchio, bok choy, and even Swiss chard, taste sweet and tender when they are picked young and small in size.

Ultimately, it's your choice whether you wish to pick leafy greens when they are big or small, but here are few harvesting methods that you can try.

1 Cut and Come Again Method.

This is the most popular way to harvest lettuce, where you pick the outer, larger leaves first and let the smaller inner leaves grow big to harvest next. This is a fantastic way to have a continuous supply of lettuce or leafy greens over time. Market gardeners often use this method to sell fresh salad greens. With this method, pick little and pick often to encourage new growth.

2 Harvesting Whole Head.

Sometimes you may want to grow a whole head of lettuce, bok choy, or napa cabbage. If you choose to harvest the whole plant, it's best to cut it at the base at soil level and leave the roots intact in the ground to break down over time.

3 Early Morning Picking.

For the sweetest, crispiest lettuce, spinach, kale, or leafy greens, make sure to harvest them early in the morning while the weather is still cool. At this time, plants will be upright and firm and not limp and droopy. They will also have a high water content (think crispy and juicy).

Storing Harvested Lettuce

When it comes to lettuce, it's of course best to harvest and eat fresh. But that's not always possible, so how do you store it so it doesn't turn slimy, smelly, and mushy?

Here's what works for me and I hope you try it too:

1 Rinse in Cold Water.

Once you harvest individual lettuce leaves, toss them into a large bowl or tub of very cold water filled with several ice cubes too. Gently swirl, swish, and flip the leaves in the water and clean away any excess dirt, debris, or bugs that might be hiding in their folds. Repeat this process at least three times or more, until all the soil has been removed. Be gentle and try not to crush the leaves.

2 Wrap in Paper Towels.

Once the lettuce leaves have been rinsed clean, use a kitchen towel or paper towels to gently pat it dry. You could use a salad spinner too if you prefer. Wrap the dried lettuce leaves in between a few paper towels and then place inside a reusable plastic bag or zippered plastic bag that is then sealed shut. If you leave the bag open, you will notice that the lettuce will lose its moisture and turn limp very quickly.

3 Store in Crisper Section of Fridge.

Store lettuce inside the crisper section of the refrigerator and avoid storing them next to fruits, such as apples and bananas, that release ethylene gas, which can make the lettuce leaves turn brown very quickly.

If you have lots of mint, wash and pat dry the leaves and lay them flat on a baking tray in your basement (cool, dry, dark place) to dry and turn into mint powder (used in tea).

Preserving Basil and Herbs

Herbs are a must have in any vegetable garden. They are not only extremely easy to grow, make superb companion plants, taste and smell amazing, but they have great medicinal value too. Why spend lots of money buying a small bundle of herbs at the grocery store, when you can grow your own and preserve them too?

It's important to know that most herbs fall into two main categories. Soft herbs, such as basil, parsley, dill, cilantro, chives, tarragon, and chervil, have tender, delicate leaves. Woody herbs like rosemary, thyme, sage, lavender, oregano, mint, marjoram, and bay laurel have thicker, woodier stems. From my experience, it's best to freeze soft herbs to capture their flavor, while it's best to dry woody herbs as they have an earthy taste. There aren't any hard and fast rules, so yes, you can do both if you wish.

1 Place in a Jar of Water.

To make soft herbs like basil, parsley, and cilantro stay fresh for up to 3 to 4 weeks after harvest, place them in a jar of water after stripping off the lower leaves, sort of like a bouquet. Change the water every 2 days and make sure that no leaves are submerged in water. I love using a beautiful vase and filling them with freshly harvested herbs. Looks good, smells good, and tastes good too!

2 Wrap in Damp Paper Towels.

Another great way to preserve both soft and woody herbs for fresh use is to wrap them inside a damp paper towel and place them in a reusable plastic bag or zipper-close plastic bag that is sealed shut. The damp towel prevents the herbs from drying out too quickly.

3 Freeze in Ice Cube Trays.

A great way to preserve herbs is by roughly chopping them and putting them inside an ice cube tray. Fill the tray with either water or an oil of your choice and freeze them. Once frozen, pop the cubes out and store in a reusable freezer-safe bag and use as needed. You can do the same with basil pesto, parsley chimichurri sauce, cilantro chutney, or chopped mint too.

Soft herbs like parsley can stay fresh for 3 to 4 weeks after harvest if you place them in a glass or vase of water. Be sure to change the water regularly and don't let the bottom leaves submerge in water.

4 Dry and Dehydrate.

Finally, the easiest way to preserve herbs for 2 to 3 years is by letting them air dry and then stripping off the leaves and storing them in an airtight glass container in a cool, dark place. You can tie herbs into little bunches or bundles after stripping off a few bottom leaves and hanging them upside down to dry. Alternatively, lay them flat on a cookie sheet and let them dry that way. It can take a few days to several weeks for herbs to air dry, depending on the type of herb, the temperature, and the level of humidity. Herbs are ready to be stored when the leaves are dry and crispy. Dried herbs last a very long time. However, their flavor and aroma diminish over time. Quick tip: Avoid washing woody herbs before drying them to help them last longer.

How to Store Potatoes for Months

Hard to find these 'Adirondack Blue' potatoes in the grocery store. Grow them yourself and you won't be disappointed.

One of the best reasons to grow the humble potato is because it stores incredibly well and can be a great source of food for your family in the cold, winter months.

1 The Ideal Storage Potato.

To ensure that your potatoes last a really long time, harvest potatoes when the leaves/foliage on the plant have turned yellow or brown and died back completely. Do not water your potato plant for at least 7 to 10 days prior to harvest.

2 How to Cure Potatoes.

After you harvest and sort through your potatoes, simply brush off excess soil that is around them. Do not wash or scrub the potatoes at this point. This process of prepping your potatoes to get them ready for storage is known as *curing*. Place your freshly harvested potatoes in a warm, dry, dark, and well-ventilated area for 1 to 2 weeks. After 2 weeks, check your potato harvest to make sure that they aren't moist or damp (in which case cure for longer) and also inspect for any rotting potatoes, which should be discarded.

3 Storing Potatoes.

Once potatoes have been cured, you can transfer them into cardboard boxes with holes poked on the sides for ventilation. Breathable mesh bags, burlap sacks, or wooden crates work too. Store in a cool, dark, well-ventilated place for 3 to 5 months. The ideal temperature for storing potatoes is between 45°F to 55°F (7°C to 13°C).

How to Store Onions and Garlic for Months

Onions and garlic are my favorite crops to grow because they are pantry essentials in most households and are so incredibly easy to grow and store.

Cure freshly harvested onions and garlic for at least 2 weeks by hanging them to dry on a drying rack or laying them flat on some cardboard.

1   The Ideal Storage Onions and Garlic.

When it comes to onions, sweet onions like 'Vidalia' and 'Walla Walla' have thinner skins and a higher moisture content, so they won't store as long as "keeping" or "storage" onions like 'Patterson' and 'Redwing'. As far as garlic is concerned, soft neck garlic varieties like 'Inchelium Red' and 'Silver White' store for a longer time when compared to hardneck varieties like 'Music' or 'German Extra Hardy'.

2   How to Cure Onions and Garlic.

After harvesting onions and garlic, you need to cure them for 2 to 3 weeks. The first step is to gently dust off any excess soil that is on the bulbs. Do not peel off the outer skin or wrapper or wash/trim the roots or stalks.

Lay your harvest flat on top of cardboard or sheets of newspaper. Alternately place them on a drying rack and allow them to hang dry.

After 2 to 3 weeks, the outer skin or wrapper will become dry and crisp. At this point, you can brush off excess soil and trim off the stalks and roots with a sharp pair of scissors, leaving just a ½" (1 cm) stub of the stalk/stem visible on top of the bulb.

3   Storage.

Store your cured onions and garlic in cardboard boxes that have been lined with paper towels or newspapers and have holes poked on the sides for ventilation/air circulation or in breathable mesh bags or milk crates. Storing them in a cool, dark place is ideal.

Adding salt to a mixture of sliced cucumbers, onions, and chilis releases the excess liquid and moisture, ensuring a crunchy/crispy texture.

Nothing better than bread and butter pickles, a.k.a. sweet pickled cucumbers.

Pickling Cucumbers

When I think of pickled cucumbers, two main varieties come to mind: dill pickles, which have a strong sour and briney taste, and bread and butter pickles, which are sweet and sour pickled cucumbers. There are many stories on the Internet about how bread and butter pickles got their name. One story goes that quick pickled cucumbers gained popularity during the Great Depression, when fresh food was scarce and ingredients such as salt and vinegar were less expensive and easily available. People grew as much as they could in their backyard kitchen gardens (also known as victory gardens) and preserved and pickled their harvests to feed their families during the lean winter months. During colder months, many families got by with just a simple sandwich made with bread and butter and slices of pickled cucumbers in between, hence the name bread and butter pickles.

If you have an abundance of cucumbers in your garden, why not make this classic American recipe and enjoy a taste of history? These pickles taste sweet, sour, and crunchy and are so delicious that you can practically eat them right out of the jar. The recipe is to the right (double the ingredients to make a bigger batch).

BREAD AND BUTTER PICKLES

Ingredients:

CUCUMBER MIX

1 pound (454 g) mini cucumbers
(or any seedless cucumber,
sliced to ¼" or 6 mm thickness)

½ small white onion, sliced

2 red chilis, de-seeded and halved

1½ tablespoons (23 g) kosher salt or
pickling salt

BRINE MIX

¾ cup (151 g) sugar

1 cup (237 ml) white distilled vinegar

⅛ cup (30 ml) water

½ tablespoon (8 g) yellow mustard seeds

½ teaspoon (3 g) dill seeds

A pinch of ground cloves (about
¹/₁₆ teaspoon)

¼ teaspoon (1 g) turmeric powder

½ teaspoon (2 g) whole black peppercorns

2 cloves garlic, sliced

How to Proceed:

1 Place sliced cucumbers, onions, and
red chilis in a bowl. Add salt. Mix.
Cover with cling wrap and put into
the refrigerator for 4 hours. Stir occasionally while in the fridge to help
incorporate salt into the ingredients.

2 After 4 hours, drain out the excess
liquid that has separated, by putting
cucumber mixture onto a sieve. Rinse
thoroughly under cold water for 3 to
4 minutes to wash off the salt.

3 Make brine by adding the brine
ingredients to a saucepan and stir
over medium heat. When liquid starts
simmering, add in the rinsed cucumber mix.

4 Bring to a simmer (this should take
2 minutes).

5 Take the pickles off the heat and let
cool.

To Store:

Once pickles have cooled to room
temperature, their color will change from
bright green to a beautiful chartreuse
green color. Transfer them to glass jars or
pickling bottles of your choice and store
in the refrigerator for up to 2 months.

Making Tomato Sauce

Want to capture the essence of summer? There's only one way—by making your own tomato sauce using homegrown tomatoes! Plum and paste tomatoes like 'San Marzano', Roma, 'Midnight Roma', and Amish Paste are the absolute best for making thick, robust sauces because they have fewer seeds, more pulp, and less water content. Select tomatoes that are ripe and at their prime so they have the maximum flavor and sweetness. This sauce is so delicious that you may just end up eating it with a spoon! The full recipe is below.

Nothing can beat the delicious flavor and freshness of homemade tomato sauce.

TOMATO SAUCE

Ingredients:

3½ pounds (1.6 kg) plum or paste tomatoes, quartered

½ cup (120 ml) water

¼ cup (60 ml) olive oil

½ medium onion, finely diced

4 small cloves garlic, minced

1 stick celery, finely diced

1 small carrot, finely diced (optional)

4 tablespoons (60 g) tomato paste

½ teaspoon dried Italian herbs

¼ teaspoon dried red chili flakes

1 teaspoon (5 ml) white wine vinegar

¼ teaspoon white miso paste

2 teaspoons sugar

Salt to taste

2 tablespoons (3 g) fresh basil leaves, julienned

2 whole fresh basil leaves (plus a few extra for garnish)

How to Proceed:

1   Wash and cut tomatoes into quarters.

2   Place the quartered tomatoes inside an instant pressure cooker along with ½ cup (118 ml) water and cook on the pressure cooker setting (on high) for 10 minutes. Release the pressure and open the lid. Majority of excess liquid would have separated from the tomatoes. Carefully scoop out the tomatoes using a slotted spoon, separating them from the liquid/broth and transfer into a bowl.

3   Reserve 1 cup (237 ml) of the tomato broth or excess liquid for cooking the sauce.

4   Let tomatoes cool for a few minutes so they are easy to handle, then peel the skin off the tomatoes (it should slip right off).

5   Crush the peeled tomatoes with your hands or with the back of the slotted spoon for a rustic, slightly chunky texture. If you want a smooth sauce, then puree the peeled tomatoes in a high-powered blender. Pass through a fine mesh sieve. Discard the seeds that may collect on the sieve.

6   Next, heat olive oil in a heavy bottom pot or Dutch oven. Add onions, celery, carrots, and a little salt and cook on a low flame/heat for 8 to 10 minutes. This will make the veggies sweat and take on a sweet, caramelized flavor. Add in garlic and cook for 1 more minute. Adding garlic too soon might burn it and make the sauce taste bitter.

7   Add tomato paste, miso paste, salt, sugar, dried Italian herbs, and chili flakes and cook for another 2 minutes.

8   Pour in the crushed tomatoes. Add vinegar, chopped basil, and more salt to taste.

9   Cook for 10 minutes on medium flame/heat, stirring occasionally. Add in a few ladlefuls of the reserved tomato broth to thin out the sauce to your liking.

To Store:

Add a few leaves of fresh basil to the bottom of a glass jar and pour the tomato sauce into it. Follow canning instructions for a water bath if you wish to preserve the sauce or store in the fridge where it can last for 5 days. You can also freeze it for up to 6 months. Serve over your favorite pasta, use it to make ratatouille, lasagna, and so much more.

These zucchini muffins are perfect for a quick breakfast on the go or even as a delicious tea-time snack.

Baking Zucchini Muffins

What do you do when you have an abundance of zucchini from your garden? Make these healthy, moist, fluffy, and delicious zucchini muffins, of course! It's an excellent option for breakfast, as a snack or at teatime. Did you know that zucchinis are not only low in fat and carbohydrates, but high in fiber and loaded with vitamins and minerals? I'm surprised that it is not a superfood, because it should be. Here's the recipe for this delicious goodness.

ZUCCHINI MUFFINS (MAKES 12 MUFFINS)

Ingredients:

2 cups (250 g) all-purpose flour

1 teaspoon baking soda

1 teaspoon baking powder

1 teaspoon cinnamon powder

1 teaspoon salt

2 eggs

⅓ cup (78 ml) vegetable oil

½ cup (100 g) granulated sugar

½ cup (97 g) brown sugar

1 tablespoon (15 ml) vanilla extract

2 cups (227 g) grated zucchini

How to Proceed:

1 Preheat the oven to 375°F (191°C), grate the zucchini, and set aside.

2 Dry Ingredients: In a large bowl, combine the flour, baking soda, baking powder, cinnamon, and salt.

3 Wet Ingredients: In a separate bowl, combine eggs, oil, sugars, and vanilla extract. Beat with a whisk.

4 Add the wet ingredients to the dry ingredients. Mix until roughly combined.

5 Remove excess water from the zucchini by wrapping the grated zucchini in a kitchen towel or paper towel and gently squeezing. You want it to be damp, not wet, nor completely dry.

6 Add zucchini to the batter. Fold it in until everything is well combined.

7 Line a cupcake tray with 12 liners.

8 Using an ice cream scooper, scoop and pour batter evenly into the 12 liners.

9 Bake for 23 minutes until a toothpick inserted in the center comes out clean.

If you have an abundance of zucchinis from your garden, then you've got to make these moist, delicious, and healthy muffins.

To Store:

Store in an airtight container at room temperature for up to 1 week. These muffins make an easy breakfast or snack on the go. Or you can even turn it into dessert by serving it warm with a scoop of vanilla bean ice cream on the side. Don't forget to add edible flowers like violas or pansies on top to impress your friends. Enjoy!

Pickled radishes are so delicious that they rarely last a week in my fridge. Add them to tacos, avocado toast, sandwiches, or tostadas or use them to garnish some simple rice and beans dishes.

Pickling Radishes

As much as I try to succession plant radishes, I invariably end up with a massive harvest each year. Radishes are one of the fastest growing vegetables and go from seed to harvest in 30 to 40 days. Some varieties like the small 'Cherry Belle' radish are ready for harvest in just 25 days.

Radishes have a sharp, spicy taste when they are raw, but when pickled in vinegar, they develop a tangy, salty, delicious flavor that's hard to resist. At right is my recipe for making pickled radishes in under 10 minutes, and I'm sure it will be your new favorite condiment.

PICKLED RADISHES

Ingredients:

10 radishes washed and trimmed (about ¼ pound or 113 g)

½ cup (118 ml) water

½ cup (118 ml) white distilled vinegar

1 tablespoon (15 g) sugar

1 teaspoon (6 g) pickling salt

1 clove garlic, smashed

1 bay leaf

¼ teaspoon (1 g) whole black peppercorns

½ teaspoon (2 g) mustard seeds

¼ teaspoon (1 g) coriander seeds

¼ teaspoon (1 g) chili flakes

How to Proceed:

1 Slice the radishes as thinly as possible. Use a mandolin if you prefer.

2 In a small pot, make a brine by adding water, vinegar, sugar, salt, garlic, bay leaf, peppercorns, mustard seeds, coriander seeds, and chili flakes. Bring the above mixture to a boil, and when it does, turn off the heat.

3 Pour the brine mixture over the sliced radishes and let it cool for 30 minutes.

4 Transfer into a glass jar and refrigerate for a few hours to let the flavors marinate in the radishes.

To Store:

Store pickled radishes in the fridge for up to 3 weeks. Use it as a topping on avocado toast, tacos, burritos, nachos, sandwiches, and so much more. Pickled radishes are a big hit when served on a charcuterie board with olives, cheese, and nuts on the side.

My favorite radish varieties to grow are 'Roxanne', Easter Egg, and 'French Breakfast' varieties.

Dried cayenne peppers can be crushed to make chili flakes or powdered to make spicy chili powder.

Chili flakes are traditionally made with red cayenne peppers; however, feel free to use any spicy peppers of choice to make your own version.

Homemade Chili Flakes

Making chili flakes and chili powder at home is so easy, you'll wonder why you didn't do it before. The flavor and heat levels will be so strong and fresh that it just won't compare to the chili flakes that you buy at the grocery store. I also found that my homemade chili flakes had the most vibrant bright red color and tasted complex, spicy, and deliciously fruity.

If you want a completely authentic experience, then grow your own spicy red pepper varieties. Cayenne pepper is the most traditional hot pepper used to make chili flakes, but of course you can use any combination of hot peppers from your garden and make your own version.

To make chili flakes, you will first need to dry or dehydrate your hot peppers. There are several ways of doing it, including slow roasting them in the oven at 180°F (82°C) for 5 to 6 hours, turning them over midway through the heating process. Another way is to string the red chilis into a garland and hang them to dry for at least a month. This looks beautiful and rustic while it hangs in a warm, dry place and the dried chilis can later be crushed to make chili flakes. Lastly, you can also use a dehydrator to crisp up your hot peppers, which is the way I do it at home. Either way, you'll have fantastic results and lots of fresh chili flakes or chili powder to use and store for months to come.

Here's how to make homemade chili flakes.

HOMEMADE CHILI FLAKES

Ingredients:

Red Cayenne Peppers

How to Proceed:

1 Wash, dry, and roughly chop the peppers. Be sure to wear gloves to protect your hands to prevent a stinging/burning sensation from the capsaicin.

2 If your peppers have too many seeds, slit the chilis in half and discard some of the seeds. Too many seeds in chili flakes can lead to an unpleasant, bitter flavor.

3 Place the chilis inside a dehydrator for 12 hours at 145°F (63°C). They should become crisp and snap easily. Depending on your location and humidity in your area, you may need to adjust the drying time. Please make sure that the dehydrator is placed in a well-ventilated location, such as your garage, deck, or patio; otherwise, the pungent smell can be too overpowering. If you choose to dry your hot peppers in the oven, then make sure the vent is turned on and windows are kept open. Don't let this process scare you because the end result is totally worth it.

4 Transfer dried chilis into a mini food processor and pulse to make chili flakes.

5 Pulverize the flakes in a coffee grinder if you wish to turn them into chili powder.

To Store:

Transfer chili flakes into an airtight container, preferably a glass bottle or reuse your old spice jars and containers that have a shaker top. Chili flakes do turn dark red in color and lose their aroma after some time, so if you want your chili flakes to stay fresh for over a year, then store the dried chilies whole and grind them with a mortar and pestle every time you want to use them in cooking. You can even store them sealed in the refrigerator too. Chili flakes and chili powder make an excellent topping for pizzas, pastas, curries, noodles, soups, stews, chili, and pretty much any recipe that calls for some spiciness. Enjoy!

Garlic Herb Butter

Use fresh herbs from your garden to make this simple and mouthwateringly delicious garlic herb butter that can be spread over breads and baguettes, or even drizzled over roasted potatoes and vegetables.

GARLIC HERB BUTTER

Ingredients:

1 stick (112 grams) unsalted butter (softened to room temperature)

½ teaspoon olive oil

1 bulb garlic

1 tablespoon (6 g) basil, finely chopped

1 tablespoon (6 g) scallions, finely chopped

1 tablespoon (3 g) chives, finely chopped

½ tablespoon (2 g) dill, finely chopped

½ tablespoon (2 g) parsley, finely chopped

Salt to taste

How to Proceed:

1   Preheat the oven to 350°F (177°C).

2   Slice off the top of the garlic bulb and drizzle it with olive oil. Make sure that some oil seeps in between the cloves too.

3   Wrap the oiled garlic bulb in aluminum foil (or place in a small Dutch oven with lid on) and pop into the preheated oven for 35 minutes.

4   In the meantime, wash, pat dry, and finely chop your fresh herbs (basil, scallions, chives, dill, and parsley).

5   Once garlic is ready and cooled to room temperature, add softened butter into a bowl and squeeze in the pulp of the roasted garlic.

6   Add chopped herbs and salt to taste and mix well with a spatula or fork to incorporate the ingredients.

To Store:

Roll the garlic herb butter in wax paper and store in the refrigerator for up to 2 weeks.

Enjoy this delicious butter by slathering it on warm breads or roasted vegetables and even as a sauce for pasta and noodles.

Crispy Naan Flatbread with Swiss Chard, Apples, and Cheese

Swiss chard is one of those delicious, nutritious veggies that looks amazing in the garden, but a lot of people don't know what to do with it except to use it in soups, stews, and stir-fries. Try making this delicious recipe and I know you'll want to grow more of it every year! The best part is that it's ready in under 20 minutes.

CRISPY NAAN FLATBREAD WITH SWISS CHARD, APPLES, AND CHEESE

Ingredients:

3 large leaves of Swiss chard slivered (stems diced into small pieces)

1 Red Delicious apple, thinly sliced (can substitute with any apples of your choice)

3 pieces garlic naan flatbread cut in half (can substitute with regular naan flatbread)

½ cup (112 g) goat cheese

A drizzle of olive oil

Salt and pepper to taste

Balsamic vinegar (optional)

How to Proceed:

1   Preheat oven to 400°F (204°C).

2   While the oven is heating, slice your chard and apples.

3   Lightly grease your baking tray and place naan bread on top.

4   Layer generously with chard and apple slices and top with cheese.

5   Drizzle a tiny bit of olive oil on top, sprinkle with salt and pepper to taste, and place in the oven for 15 to 20 minutes. The bottom of the flatbread will turn brown and crispy by then.

Drizzle some balsamic vinegar on top. Serve warm with a glass of chilled kombucha on the side.

One of the main reasons why my backyard vegetable garden has been thriving for over 5 years is because I've invested my time, energy, and resources into having the best quality soil I possibly can.

Chapter 7

SUPERCHARGE YOUR SOIL

G ood soil is really the foundation, heart, and core of a vegetable garden. Here's what constitutes good soil:

1   Texture (20 percent clay, 40 percent sand, and 40 percent silt)

2   Organic Matter (right amount of macro- and micronutrients, compost, and amendments)

3   PH (6.5 to 7 is the ideal pH for most plants)

If there is one place where I want you to invest a maximum amount of time, effort, and resources into, it's on creating the best soil possible for your garden. The first place to start is by conducting a soil test. It will help guide you on what type of amendments to add to your garden so that plants can be as healthy and happy as possible.

Please keep in mind that, generally speaking, most plants like a slightly acidic soil with a pH of around 6.5 to 7 and soil that is loamy in consistency (the right balance of sand and clay). In this chapter, you will learn different ways to test your soil, including a DIY method that you can try at home.

You will also learn about the importance of compost, how to make your own using kitchen scraps, and how to apply it to your garden.

Finally, I will show you how to easily amend your existing garden soil (you don't have to throw it out each season) and how to add a variety of different organic ingredients, such as eggshells, coffee grounds, and mushroom compost in order to build healthy soil that is teeming with a diverse variety of beneficial microbes and soil biology.

Testing Your Soil

Every 3 to 4 years, it's a great idea to get your garden soil tested for nutrient levels and pH values. As plants grow in the same soil season upon season, they absorb the nutrients from the soil, leaving it lackluster and depleted. This can often create nutrient imbalances, which can affect the growth of subsequent crops. Most gardeners think that adding fertilizers to the soil will fix the problem, and it can help to a certain extent. However, it's really important to take the guesswork out of gardening and conduct a soil test to determine the quality of your growing medium. Here are a few easy ways to test the soil in your vegetable garden.

1   Contact Your Local Cooperative Extension.

The best, most reliable way to conduct a soil test is to contact your local cooperative extension agency, which is usually affiliated with a local university. Simply search on the Internet for "local cooperative extension office near me" and a few results should pop up. These offices are usually affiliated with local counties and the National Institute of Food and Agriculture (NIFA) and their goal is to empower farmers, growers, and local communities and support them in their efforts to grow food.

When you contact your local cooperative extension office, they will most likely ask you to send them a few samples of your soil, taken from different parts of your garden. They will then give you the results of the test, which will tell you what your soil is deficient in and what it has an excess of. These tests are quite comprehensive and will give you not just the macronutrient profile of your soil (N, P, and K values) but also the micronutrients too (such as calcium, magnesium, iron, zinc, sodium, etc.).

2   Buy a Soil Testing Kit.

Another great way to conduct a soil test is by purchasing a kit from a local gardening center or big box retailer. There are different types of kits available—some can tell you about the macronutrient levels in your soil (nitrogen, phosphorus, and potassium), others can find out the pH value (acidic or alkaline), while some others can even tell you moisture levels too. While these tests may not be as accurate as a comprehensive test done by a lab, it will still give you a general idea about the condition of your soil. These tests are usually more expensive than sending a sample to your local cooperative extension; however, you can know the results fairly quickly. Some companies like MySoil will even send you a kit where you send your soil sample and mail it to them for detailed analysis and recommendations.

3 DIY Soil Test.

Did you know that good soil is made up of 20 percent clay, 40 percent sand, and 40 percent silt? A great way to check the texture of your soil is by doing an easy DIY Mason Jar Test at home. All you need are a mason jar, sifted soil sample, water, ruler, or measuring tape and a marker. Head to your garden and dig 6 inches (15 cm) deep and collect a sample at this depth. Repeat for several locations. Sift the collected soil to remove rocks and big chunks of debris and fill one-third of a mason jar with it. Add water into the jar to fill it up to its shoulders. Close the lid and shake the jar really well. Place on a flat surface and let it rest.

After 1 minute, mark and measure the amount of sand that has settled at the bottom. This will be the sand in your soil. After another 4 minutes, mark and measure the sediment again. The dif ference between the new measurement and the old one will be the amount of silt in the soil. After 24 hours, mark and measure the sediment level once again. The difference between this third level and the second level will be the amount of clay in your soil.

DIY Soil Test: Collect samples of soil from different areas of the garden. Sift it into a mason jar, add water, and let it sit. This type of soil test will reveal the amount of clay, sand, and silt in your soil.

You can amend a heavy clay soil by adding more coarse sand and compost, while sandy soil can be fixed by adding more compost and humus. If your soil is high in silt, add in coarse sand and composted manure, which will help amend it over time.

Refresh soil for a new growing season by discarding dying and diseased crops and removing any weeds and fruits that might have fallen on the soil.

Add compost or good quality organic bagged soil as a last layer on top of your raised beds before planting.

How to Refresh/Amend Existing Soil

Did you know that you don't need to toss out old soil from your raised beds and containers each year? There are easy ways to refresh and reuse existing soil, save some money, and grow healthy plants in your vegetable garden. The only time you may want to replace your soil is if plants that have been growing there were ridden with pests and diseases that are soil borne or can overwinter in the soil. Even in that case, you could try crop rotation before you discard old soil. Here's how to refresh, amend, and reuse existing soil.

1 Remove Existing Plants and Debris.

When refreshing your soil each season and to get your garden prepped and ready for planting, the first step is to remove existing spent plants and any dried and diseased leaves and fruits that may have fallen on the ground.

2 Should You Remove Roots?

If you're growing in containers, then yes, it is important to pull the plant out by the roots and remove fibrous root matter. This is because a container has very limited growing space and new plants/seedlings need space and soil for their own root systems to grow and develop. If you're growing in raised beds, then you do not need to remove the plant by its roots. Instead, you can snip off the plant at the base or soil level and leave the roots in the soil to decompose over time and feed soil life.

3 Loosen Existing Soil.

After removing plant matter and any debris, it's important to loosen up the soil and aerate it as soil does tend to compact and compress over time. To do this, simply use a rake to gently lift and turn the top few inches of soil. Fluffing up soil this way is also important when planting root crops like carrots for a perfect harvest each time.

4 Apply Compost of Bagged Soil.

Once your raised beds and containers have been prepped, it's time to add compost or good quality bagged organic soil that's high in organic matter. I always top my beds this way each season so new seedlings have fresh soil and nutrients to start growing in. Also over time, as plants get bigger and as you water or when it rains, the nutrients slowly seep down to the root level, becoming available for plants to absorb.

5 Sprinkle Granular Fertilizer.

Finally, as a last step, I always sprinkle a few handfuls of granular organic fertilizer on top of the soil/compost and gently scratch it in. Any all-purpose organic fertilizer will do. Just make sure that it has a balanced amount of macronutrients such as an NPK of 5-5-5 or 3-3-3.

Mushroom compost is the composted medium in which mushrooms are grown. Its texture resembles mulch and I use it to side-dress my garlic and carrot plants in fall.

Leaf mold is an excellent soil conditioner and easy to make from dried leaves that have fallen in your yard.

Adding Diversity to Your Soil

Each autumn I try to add different types of compost or organic matter to my soil—one year it's homemade compost, next year I might add mushroom compost, and another year it will be leaf mold or leaf compost. This not only adds different nutrients to the soil but truly helps build a diverse and rich soil biology that greatly boosts the overall health of the garden. Like they say, "Eat the rainbow," I say feed the soil a wide variety of nutrient-rich organic amendments to encourage biodiversity because ultimately, if your soil is healthy, your plants will be healthy and you'll be happy too.

Some of the different types of compost are composted horse manure, composted chicken manure, vermicompost, composted food scraps or kitchen wastes, mushroom compost, and leaf mold. Here are my top three favorites.

1 Mushroom Compost.

Did you know that mushroom compost is not composted or broken-down mushrooms, but in fact it is the growing medium in which mushrooms are cultivated? Mushrooms are usually grown in composted bales of straw or hay, mixed with poultry or horse manure, and can have additives like peat moss, lime, gypsum, potash, cottonseed meal, soybean meal, etc. After mushrooms are harvested, the compost in which they were grown is broken down at high temperatures over many weeks, killing weed seeds or pathogens that may be present.

Mushroom compost may not be as nutrient rich as homemade compost, but it still has plenty of nutrients left over that make it ideal for a vegetable garden. It has a wonderful texture, which makes it a great material to mulch with. It helps to suppress weeds and I love using it to mulch around my garlic and carrots in fall, with great success.

A word of caution though: Since it's slightly high in soluble salts, only apply to the garden every 2 to 3 years. Also, try to find out the source of the mushroom compost, to ensure that it is organic and that animal manures used are free of antibiotics or hormones.

2 Leaf Mold.

Another fantastic soil conditioner for your vegetable garden is leaf mold, which is nothing but composted leaves. It is fungal-dominated compost that not only adds organic matter to the soil but makes an excellent habitat for earthworms and beneficial bacteria too. The best part is you can make this yourself for free!

To make leaf mold, collect dry, fallen leaves around your property in autumn and place them inside a large garbage bag. Poke several holes at the bottom of the bag for aeration. Moisten the leaves with some water and then tie/close the bag shut.

Leaves will take at least a year to break down and turn into rich, black leaf mold. However, you can speed up the composting process by chopping leaves into smaller pieces using a leaf shredding machine.

I add a 2- to 3-inch (5 to 8 cm) thick layer on top of my existing soil in autumn and let it break down further over the winter months.

3 Homemade Compost.

Finally, my absolute favorite amendment to add to my garden: homemade compost made from food wastes/kitchen scraps. This is something you can add anytime and all the time too if you wish; however, I do like alternating it with the other different composts mentioned above to add that diversity to my soil. I usually recommend adding it to your garden in fall and spring. Add 2 to 3 inches (5 to 8 cm) on top of your soil. You can even side-dress your plant with it in summer too if you generate enough. Read on to learn how to make your own compost.

Making Compost

Not enough good things can be said about homemade compost! Hands down composting is the best practice for the environment and for your garden too. Lots of people feel overwhelmed by the thought of composting, but it's really quite simple, especially if you start with a tumbling-style composter with two compartments.

1   The Setup.

First, invest in a small kitchen pail with a carbon liner in its lid. This will be used to collect all your kitchen scraps. Do not add meat, fat, dairy, or cooked food into it. Also purchase a tumbling-style composter and place it in your backyard or near your garden. If this is your first time, you will also need a compost starter or actual compost to kick start or ignite the process.

2   The Technique.

There are only four main inputs that are needed to make great compost: greens, browns, air, and water. Please see the chart below to see what constitutes green and brown material.

Green Materials (high in Nitrogen)	Brown Materials (high in Carbon)
Kitchen scraps such as fruit and vegetable peels, tea leaves, coffee grounds, stale bread, juice pulp, grass clippings (no pesticides or chemicals please), green leaves/green plant material (that is free of diseases and pests)	Dried leaves, shredded paper (avoid magazines with chemical dyes/inks), shredded cardboard, dried twigs and branches, sawdust, wood shavings, pine pellets

My composting setup starts with a kitchen pail where I collect fruit and vegetable peels, coffee grounds, and juicing remnants.

Fresh compost made in my tumbling-style composter.

In order to successfully make great compost, the ratio of green to brown materials needs to be 1:3 or 1:4 in volume, NOT weight. What does that mean? It means if you add 1 gallon (3.8 L) of green material, you will need to add 3 to 4 gallons (11.5 to 15 L) of brown material into your composter.

Please keep in mind that the smaller or finer the materials, the quicker they will break down and turn into compost, so chop up your materials into smaller bits if you can.

When you collect a sufficient amount of green and brown materials, add them into one compartment of your composter and add the compost starter or a few shovelfuls of compost to ignite the process. Spin your composter five times and make sure to turn the composter at least 3 days a week for aeration (yes, even in winter). Keep adding your materials into the same compartment until it gets full. Then start adding into the other empty compartment. As the materials break down, you will notice that the volume shrinks down significantly. And that's okay. In fact, that's great. It means that the compost is "cooking" or doing its thing. Do not be tempted to add fresh material into the chamber that's cooking as it will slow down the process significantly.

In 4 to 5 months, you should have beautiful finished compost that looks like fluffy rich soil and smells like the Earth, ready to apply in your garden.

Don't add whole eggshells directly into your composter. They take years to break down.

Using Eggshells and Coffee Grounds in the Garden

Eggshells and coffee grounds are wonderful natural and free amendments for your organic vegetable garden and I do recommend using them. However, there are a lot of misconceptions about what they can or cannot do and how to use them effectively. Two of the most common myths are that crushed eggshells will keep slugs away (not true) and that coffee grounds will make your soil very acidic (most of the acid gets washed away into the coffee you drink). Read on to learn about how to properly use these fantastic amendments in ways that will actually benefit your plants.

1   Pulverize Eggshells and Add to Compost Pile.

Eggshells are an incredible source of calcium as they contain a high amount of calcium carbonate. It's an amendment that you may want to add, especially if your tomatoes are showing signs of blossom end rot. Unfortunately, eggshells take a really long time to break down (over 2 to 3 years) and the calcium isn't readily available for plants to absorb. To speed up that process, pulverize washed, dried, and baked eggshells in a coffee grinder or high-speed blender and add that powder to your compost pile or worm bin to further decompose over time. (Baking eggshells in the oven for 10 to 15

Pulverize eggshells into a fine powder and then add it into your compost bin. Earthworms like its gritty texture too.

minutes at 200°F or 93°C helps reduce the risk of salmonella). Add this supercharged compost to your garden each year and you'll never have to worry about calcium deficiency again.

2   Eggshells and Vinegar Recipe for Quick Release Calcium.

If you want calcium to be readily available for your plants, then mix equal amounts of pulverized eggshells with distilled white vinegar (1:1 ratio). Let it steep for 1 hour. You will see bubbling and frothing as the acid in the vinegar dissolves the calcium carbonate in the eggshells and makes it bio-available. Don't worry: The calcium neutralizes the acid (resulting in a neutral PH). Add 4 tablespoons (60 ml) of this mixture to 1 gallon (3.8 L) of water and water your plants with it.

3   Sprinkle Coffee Grounds for Nitrogen-Loving Plants.

Coffee grounds are an excellent source of nitrogen for your vegetable garden and break down in just 3 to 4 months (much faster than eggshells). I personally prefer to add it to my compost pile so it can break down quickly thanks to heat from the compost and worm activity. However, it's fine to sprinkle it around the base of your plants and lightly rake it in as well. Just don't expect any immediate results from it as it will take a few months to release nitrogen into the soil.

I'm able to double my harvests and grow-ing season in New Jersey by covering my raised beds with 6-mil farm-grade plastic over hoops.

Chapter 8

EXTEND YOUR GROWING SEASON

Growing food in the garden when the weather is below freezing, sometimes snowing, and when people think plants can't survive is what makes fall/winter gardening most exciting to me. Life wants to live and a garden wants to grow, and if you just give it a little help with some season extension tips and tricks, you'll be happily harvesting food even when you thought it wasn't possible.

Most people think that their gardening season lies between their last and first frost dates, but nothing could be further from the truth. While heat-loving summer crops such as tomatoes, cucumbers, peppers, and eggplants will die with a hard frost, several cold-hardy varieties will grow and thrive in the colder months, in below freezing temperatures. Read the section "What Crops Can Grow in the Snow?" to find out all the varieties of vegetables that love growing in the cold.

To extend your growing season, you don't need to spend lots of money on expensive greenhouses and fancy setups. In fact, even simple household items such as clear plastic bins can work as makeshift covers (place a brick on top to keep them from flying away in the wind).

The key to successfully harvesting food well past your first frost date is to ensure that cold-hardy crops are big and well established before snow and winter arrives. This means that cool-season veggies need to be planted between late summer and early fall. Small seedlings have a low chance of success. However, stronger, larger plants with well-established root systems can withstand the cold better.

In the section "Why You Should Be Growing Food in Fall and Winter," I will encourage and inspire you to grow your own fall/winter vegetable garden. If you choose not to grow food in the colder months, that's okay too. Just don't leave your soil bare. Instead cover it with organic matter or cover crops that will boost soil health so that your garden wakes up refreshed and renewed in spring.

Cold-hardy veggies that have been touched by frost taste incredibly sweet and delicious.

Fall is one of my favorite gardening seasons as pest pressure is very low and the cool, pleasant weather makes gardening chores enjoyable.

Why You Should Be Growing Food in Fall and Winter

One of the reasons why fall/winter is a wonderful time to grow food is because the weather is so enjoyable (no sweating under the hot sun while gardening). Also, the garden doesn't need as much care and switches to autopilot or survival mode as temperatures start to drop, which means less work for you as a gardener. If that doesn't convince you, here are more enticing reasons why you should be growing food in the colder months.

1 Low Pest Pressure.

As the weather starts cooling down, you will notice that pest pressure greatly reduces. In summer we can get tired of battling aphids, mealybugs, blight, and spider mites, but in fall/winter these pests go into hibernation and you can enjoy sweet lettuces, crispy bok choy, and hardy kale without constantly worrying about controlling pests and diseases. One word of caution: Yes, aphids and cabbage moths can be a problem in late summer and early fall when the cool-season garden has just been planted and the weather is still warm. However, you can simply wash off aphids with a jet of water and use row covers and organic Bt to control cabbage loopers. Once temperatures are in the 40s and 30s°F and below (4°C to -1°C), these pests won't be a problem.

2 Low to No Watering Needed.

Did you know that you rarely need to water your vegetable garden in winter? The reason for this is that as temperatures cool down, plant growth slows down significantly and eventually stops temporarily. Plants' need for water reduces greatly. Also when temperatures drop below 45°F or 7°C, I cover my cold-hardy plants in my raised beds with hoops and 6-mil farm-grade plastic. This creates a mini greenhouse or terrarium effect inside. As plants transpire, they release water vapor, which hits the cold plastic and falls back down as rain, keeping the soil moist. The only time I'd water my winter garden is if we have unusually warm weather or if the soil seems dry to touch.

3 Sweet Tasting Veggies.

One of the absolute best reasons to grow food in fall and winter is that the veggies actually taste so much sweeter than when they are grown in warmer months. Carrots, lettuce, even kale, and broccoli taste sweet like candy once they've been touched by frost. This is because the cold temperature causes the plant to convert starches into sugars as a survival mechanism. The sweetness in flavor is so pronounced that I only grow carrots in fall as the ones grown in spring and summer seem bland and tasteless in comparison.

What Crops Can Grow in the Snow?

Now we come to the best part—what can you grow, even in the snow? Before you read about the varieties to plant, it's important to know how and when to plant them. As temperatures start to drop and sunlight hours start reducing in fall and winter in the northern hemisphere, plant growth slows down significantly and sometimes even stops completely. The key to harvesting food in the snow is to ensure that plants are significantly large and well established as they head into the cold winter months, to give them a fighting chance of survival. Finally, add some mulch and a layer of cover or protection to keep the plants warm and toasty.

1 Super Cold-Hardy Crops.

Different crops have varying degrees of tolerance to the cold. Some are super cold hardy, while others can only tolerate a light frost. The plants that you choose to grow in your winter garden will depend on your weather and climatic conditions and the type of cover or protection that you provide. Super cold-hardy crops that can survive temperatures below 28°F (-2°C) are spinach, kale, cilantro, parsley, mustards, radishes, carrots, cabbage, broccoli, Brussels sprouts, collards, leeks, parsnips, turnips, and garlic. Garlic is the only crop that doesn't need protection/cover at all.

2 Semi-Cold-Hardy Veggies.

Semi-cold-hardy crops that can survive temperatures between 28°F to 32°F (-2°C to 0°C) are beets, Swiss chard, arugula, lettuce, bok choy, napa cabbage, fenugreek, and scallions. These veggies have tender leaves and hence cannot tolerate very low temperatures.

3 Tips for Growing in the Snow.

To maximize harvests in the snow, cover your raised beds with hoops and 6-mil clear farm-grade plastic and secure them with clips so the plastic is taunt and doesn't fly away in the wind. I cover my crops when temperatures are below 45°F (7°C). I open up/uncover the plastic in early fall or when daytime temperatures are above 45°F (7°C). When it comes to the plastic cover, make sure that it goes all the way to the bottom or base of your raised beds, so it doesn't flap around on a cold, windy day. If cold wind enters inside, it will give the plants a chill and dry out the soil. You can, of course, open the plastic when you want to harvest, but close it after that again to regulate the temperature inside.

Despite the snow, I was able to harvest kale, bok choy, cilantro, lettuce, carrots, radishes, arugula, beets, and Swiss chard from my New Jersey garden in December.

Pushing the limits of what you can grow even when it's cold outside is what makes nature so amazing.

Finally, if you do experience a heavy snowfall, don't forget to head into your garden once it stops and wipe all that snow off the top of the plastic covers so sunlight can filter in.

Lots of plants will die if temperatures consistently stay in the teens and single digits (Fahrenheit) for over 5 to 7 days. Some plants might look like their foliage is frozen and dead on top. However, their root systems will still be alive and they will grow back again first thing in spring as soon as temperatures start warming up.

Cold-Hardy Vegetables

Leafy Greens	Arugula, claytonia, corn salad, fenugreek, mache, mustards, spinach, Swiss chard, vetch
Brassicas	Bok choy, broccoli, Brussels sprouts, cabbage, cauliflower, collards, kale, kohlrabi, leeks
Root Vegetables	Beets, carrots, parsnips, radish, turnips
Herbs	Chives, cilantro, lavender, oregano, parsley, rosemary, thyme

Extending the Growing Season

There are several materials and fabrics that you can use to extend your growing season. What you choose depends on your weather during the coldest months. Someone with mild winters can get away with using fleece fabric or a light frost cloth to cover their plants at night. For someone else who has a garden in a colder region, a cold-frame greenhouse or high tunnel is a must to be successful at winter gardening.

For season extension success, start with using lighter fabrics like fleece fabric or frost blankets in early fall (especially at night when temperatures dip below 50°F or 10°C) and then switch to heavier, less porous materials like 6-mil farm-grade plastic when temperatures drop below 45°F (7°C).

Here are some tips to help you grow food as temperatures start to get cold.

1   Mulch.

It's crucial to mulch your garden in fall/winter. Mulch has three benefits: One, it keeps the soil moist and helps retain water. Second, it insulates your soil, keeping the roots of your plants warm and comfortable and prevents the ground from freezing. Last, mulches like mushroom compost or even dried leaves add organic matter to the soil and fertilize cold-hardy plants in the cooler months.

2   Fleece Fabric and Frost Blankets.

Fleece fabric and frost blankets are thin, breathable materials that can protect your crops from frost damage. They are generally draped over the crops and allow air and water to pass through. They come in a variety of sizes and thickness (also known as gauge).

3   My Winter Setup: Hoops and Farm-Grade Plastic.

When you live in an area that gets significant amounts of snow and temperatures that dip into the 20s, teens, and even a few days in single-digit degrees Fahrenheit (-6°C and below), you need to bring out 6-mil clear farm-grade plastic or thicker. Did you know that just one layer of plastic creates enough warmth that it raises the inside temperatures by 1 to 1½ zones? You can add two layers of farm-grade plastic for a higher degree of protection. I install hoops in my raised bed using 10-foot-long, ½-inch-thick (3 m-long, 1 cm-thick) EMT pipes that I bend into hoops using a hoop bender and use ½ inch (1 cm) snap clamps to prevent the plastic from flying away in the wind. This setup keeps the plastic taunt and prevents it from bowing and bending from the snow.

Installing hoops made from 10-feet-long (3 m) electrical metal conduit pipes that are ½-inch (1 cm) thick and bent using a hoop bender. I install 3 hoops in my 4′ × 4′ (1.2 m × 1.2 m) raised bed for structural integrity.

Covering hoops with 6-mil farm-grade plastic once temperatures start dropping below 45°F (7°C).

Secure the plastic and prevent it from flying away by adding three snap clamps over each hoop: one in the middle and two on either side. Make sure the plastic is taut and tight so it doesn't collapse under the weight of snow.

Make sure that the farm-grade plastic goes all the way to the ground so cold air cannot get inside the raised beds, dry out the soil, and freeze the plants.

4   Cold Frames.

Cold frames are slanting structures with transparent tops made of glass or an old windowpane that creates a greenhouse effect inside and keeps the plants warm and thriving. Cold frames help with extending harvests in the winter and are excellent for planting seedlings much earlier in spring too.

I rarely water my fall/winter garden. Plants growing inside transpire. Their water vapor hits the cold plastic and falls back down as rain, keeping the soil moist and the cycle of life going.

Should I Water My Winter Garden?

As temperatures start getting colder and hours of sunlight go down, plant growth slows down significantly and sometimes even stops. Because of reduced cellular activity, a plant's need for water greatly reduces in winter. One of the biggest advantages of winter gardening is that you don't have to water your vegetable garden as often as you do in summer. In fact, if you're growing in a cold frame or hoop house, under the cover of farm-grade plastic, you may not need to water your plants in winter at all.

1   Only Water When Soil Is Dry.

Sometimes you can have an unusually warm winter or a few days of high temperatures. On days when temperatures are over 45°F (7°C), I open the plastic covers that are on my raised beds and allow the plants to enjoy the sunshine and pleasant air. Anytime plants are exposed to wind/breeze, the moisture in the soil will tend to evaporate or dry out. Hence, check the soil by touching it with your hands, and if it's dry, then give the plants a drink of water with some earth worm casting tea added in for gentle nutrition.

2   Water at the Soil Level.

When it comes to winter gardening, you want to make sure that you water only at the soil level and avoid getting the foliage wet. If leaves are wet, they will easily freeze

Only water the covered winter garden if soil is dry to the touch and plants look thirsty. Water only in the morning and at soil level.

when temperatures drop. This means that you will lose your harvest completely, or if you do manage to salvage some of it, it won't store well.

3   Create a Mini Greenhouse to Reduce Watering.

Using clear 6-mil farm-grade plastic draped tightly over hoops will allow you to maximize harvests from the garden and minimize watering greatly. Using this method in my outdoor raised bed garden, I'm able to double my growing season from 5 months (May to October) to 10 months (March to January) in New Jersey, zone 6B. In the colder months of November, December, and January, I rarely need to water my garden, unless we have unusually warm weather.

The combination of plastic, hoops, and snap clamps creates a mini greenhouse or low tunnel, so cold air can't get in, but sunlight is still able to filter through. Also, plants transpire and release water vapor into the air, which hits the cold plastic, condenses, and falls back down as rain, keeping the soil moist and the plants thriving.

Should I Cover the Soil in Winter?

It's the end of the gardening season, and I know you're probably tired and need a break from gardening all year long. But before you take a break, make sure that you don't leave your soil bare in winter. Instead, I highly encourage you to cover it with organic matter or cover crops so you can prevent soil and nutrient erosion and let the garden rest and regenerate so it's ready for planting come spring. Here are four ways to protect your soil over the cold months.

1   Leaf Mulch.

Leaf mulch is nothing but composted brown leaves. It is an excellent soil conditioner, adds organic matter back into the soil, earthworms love it, and the best part is that you can make it yourself for free. Read "Adding Diversity to Your Soil" on page 164 to learn how to make your own leaf mulch using dried leaves that have fallen in your backyard in autumn. Add a 2- to 3-inch-thick (5 to 8 cm) layer on top of your existing soil or mix it into the top 6 inches (15 cm) of your soil and let it break down further over the winter months. The wonderful part is that the leaf mulch will protect and delay your soil/ground from freezing in winter and will help it warm up quickly in spring (which translates into a longer growing season for you).

2   Compost.

Cover your soil with 2 to 3 inches (5 to 8 cm) of compost each fall. It's an excellent amendment for adding organic matter and nutrients back into the soil over the winter months. Plus, it helps loosen up heavy clay soil and helps with preventing water runoff in sandy soil as well. It also provides a home and habitat for soil life and beneficial insects such as earthworms to thrive. Earthworms help break down the compost further and leave behind their castings, which acts as an excellent natural fertilizer that plants love.

3   Keep Roots Intact.

At the end of the gardening season, avoid the temptation to clear your raised beds or garden and pull out all the plants by the roots. Leaving the roots intact provides food in the cold winter months for soil life to flourish underneath. This helps with soil fertility and aeration as well. Simply snip off plants at the base or soil level. In fact, if you have some plants that have flowered and gone to seed, let them stay in your garden to provide a source of food for birds and wildlife in winter.

Cover the soil and mulch your garden with organic matter like dried leaves if you don't have access to any other resources.

Composted dried leaves turn into leaf mold, which is a superb soil conditioner for the organic vegetable garden. Add it as a layer on top of existing soil or mix it into the top 6" (15 cm) of soil—both methods work.

4 Cover Crops.

Plant cover crops like oats, buckwheat, hairy vetch, winter rye, peas, clover, or alfalfa in your garden 2 to 4 weeks before your first frost date. Cover crops from the legume family fix nitrogen from the atmosphere and add it back into the soil. They are also great for suppressing weeds and don't need to be covered in winter.

The way to plant cover crops is to broadcast sow them. Densely sprinkle them on your soil/raised beds and once they grow several inches tall, you can chop and drop them on top of the soil, like you would with mulch (leave the roots intact under the ground of course).

Many farmers often use cover crops as a crop rotation strategy to add back essential nutrients like nitrogen that may have been depleted during the growing season.

How to Put the Garden to Bed

As the growing season comes to an end, it's important to prepare it for winter to ensure that your garden is refreshed and ready for planting in spring. Here are some important tasks to complete to put your garden to bed.

1   Garden Clean Up.

It's important to clean out the vegetable garden at the end of the season to prevent unwanted pests and predators from finding a home in your garden. Remove dead and decaying plants, fallen fruits, and debris. Compost what you can and burn or discard anything that's diseased. Clean out empty pots and containers, stack them up, and store them in your shed or garage in winter.

2   Turn Off Drip Irrigation/Disconnect Hose Pipes from Water Spout.

Water freezes in winter, so be sure to turn off your drip irrigation system and drain and disconnect watering hoses or pipes from the waterspout so they don't burst.

3   Clean Your Tools.

Don't forget to give your hard-working garden tools a good scrub and wash with warm water and soap before storing them away for winter. If they are rusted, you can soak them overnight in some distilled white vinegar, which will dissolve the rust. Use a steel wool pad and soap and water to clean the rust off. Wipe and dry tools with a soft cloth dipped in some vegetable oil. To disinfect tools that were in contact with diseased plants, you can simply wipe them with disinfecting wipes or a cloth that's dipped in 70 percent isopropyl alcohol.

4   Add Compost or Plant Cover Crops.

One of the most important tasks when you put your garden to bed is to add 2 to 3 inches (5 to 8 cm) of compost on top of your soil. Don't mix it in. Instead, let it be the last layer on top of your soil after clearing out dead plant matter and debris. You can also cover your soil with mulch or clean straw if you like so that it warms up quickly in spring. Alternatively, you can plant cover crops to regenerate your soil and add nutrients back into the garden.

Before a hard frost arrives, transplant some of your favorite herbs like basil into a well-draining pot and bring them indoors to enjoy all winter long.

Don't forget to thoroughly clean and disinfect your favorite gardening tools, sharpen the blades, remove the rust, and store them away for winter.

5   Bring Frost Tender Plants Indoors for Winter.

It's a great idea to take cuttings of your favorite herbs like basil, rosemary, and mint and grow them indoors to enjoy all winter long. It's very easy to root these cuttings in water for a few weeks and then transplant them into small individual containers and grow them on a sunny windowsill. Before bringing any plants indoors for winter, make sure to inspect them thoroughly for pests and diseases, hose down the leaves with water, and add some earthworm castings for gentle organic nutrition so the plants can thrive in their new environment.

Acknowledgments

First and foremost, I want to say the biggest thank you to my Mom and Dad for being my #1 fans and supporters! Your unwavering love and encouragement gave me the confidence to believe in myself and become who I am today. I'll love you forever.

To my dearest hubby, Abi: Thank you for always being there for me, believing in my capabilities, and supporting me despite my penchant of sneaking too many plants into the house!

My darling kids Aria and Aryan: I love you both too much! Aria, thank you for taking the best photos of me and the garden and baking the most delicious zucchini muffins! Aryan, thanks for being my "Momager" and giving me the best advice on social media strategy, growing my Instagram, and marketing my book.

To Rasesh Mama: You inspired me to grow my own food and sparked my love for gardening! You were my first garden teacher and mentor and so generously shared your knowledge with me. Thank you!

To my clients: Biggest thank you to Rachel and Josh Kalafer, Jamie and Brian Stelter, Cara Silman, Tisha and Ken, Jocelyn Dannenbaum, Meena Seenivasan, Kristen and Zachary Cohen, Jaclyn Pien, and so many others who ordered a garden consult with me and trusted my vision for their spaces. I am deeply grateful to you for giving me the opportunity to grow and bloom.

To Ashley: Dearest friend, thank you for connecting me with the publishers. Without you, this book would probably still be a dream for me.

To Sofia Tomé and Jessica Hendrix: You made me and my garden look gorgeous despite the sweltering July heat. Thank you so much!

To Iris: Thank you for helping me care for my garden and making it look its best.

To Bernard Bunag: Thank you for your expert craftsmanship and building the raised bed for my book.

To Jessica, David, Steve, Liz, and the Quarto team: Thank you for taking a chance on me and guiding me through the process of writing my first book!

And last but not the least, to my social media friends and followers: Thank you for hitting the "like," "follow," and "subscribe" buttons and welcoming me into your gardens virtually each day! I genuinely owe it all to you! I've written this book with you in mind—to answer the gardening questions that you've asked me over the years. Your love, trust, and support has made this book possible. Thank you from the bottom of my heart for making me a better gardener.

About the Author

Resh Gala is a self-taught organic gardener who lives in New Jersey with her family. She has an MBA in marketing and business strategy and is the founder and owner of the minority- and woman-owned business, Hundred Tomatoes, LLC. She designs and installs edible, organic gardens for clients in New Jersey, Pennsylvania, and New York, US, and consults/coaches aspiring gardeners around the world. Her work has been featured in *New Jersey Monthly* magazine, The BReeze, and she was named a gardener of the year by Burpee Home Gardens in 2020.

Although born in the US, Resh spent her childhood years growing up in Bangalore, India, where her family still resides.

Resh's mission is to encourage people to grow their own food and live their best lives, and she hopes to inspire others through her own gardening journey.

Find Resh here:
Website: reshgala.com
Instagram: @reshgala and @hundredtomatoes
YouTube: youtube.com/@reshgala
Twitter: @resh_gala
Email: info@reshgala.com
Threads: @reshgala

Photo Credits

Resh Gala: 7 (both), 8, 10, 13 (both), 19 (left), 22 (top left, top right), 24 (both), 27 (right), 34, 39 (right), 45 (both), 48, 49, 50, 52, 54, 59, 63 (both), 64, 68 (right), 76, 75, 78 (both), 81 (right), 82, 83, 84, 85 (both), 86 (both), 89, 90 (both), 93 (both), 95 (all), 97 (all), 98, 100 (both), 102 (left), 107 (left), 109 (left), 112 (both), 114, 116 (left), 118, 121 (both), 123, 124 (left), 127 (both), 129 (both), 130 (right), 134, 138, 139, 140 (both), 142, 143, 144 (left), 145, 146 (both), 148, 151, 152, 153, 154 (both), 158, 161, 162 (both), 167 (both), 172 (right), 175 (left), 178

Jessica Hendrix Puff: 11, 19 (right), 27 (left), 39 (left), 47 (left), 57 (all), 58, 60 (both), 70 (both), 73 (left), 104, 122, 136

Sofia Alexander Antunes Tomé: 15 (both), 16 (both), 21 (all), 22 (middle, bottom), 23 (all), 29 (both), 31 (both), 32 (both), 42 (both), 47 (right), 55, 66, 67, 68 (left), 73 (right), 77, 81 (left), 88, 102 (right), 105, 107 (right), 109 (right), 110, 124 (right), 130 (left), 144 (right), 150, 164 (right), 168, 169, 170, 172 (left), 177 (all), 179, 181, 183 (both)

Aria Saksena: 116 (right), 164 (left), 175 (right), 185

Shutterstock: 133 (both)

Index